TORO

© 1998 Lunwerg Editors
© text: Joaquín Vidal
© photography: Ramón Masats

Copyright © 1999 for this English edition
Könemann Verlagsgesellschaft mbH
Bonner Str. 126, D-50968 Cologne

Translated from Spanish by Lucilla Watson
Edited and typeset by Book Creation Services, Ltd.

Production Manager: Detlev Schaper
Assistant: Nicola Leurs
Printing and Binding: Mateu Cromo

Printed in Spain

ISBN: 3-8290-2230-1

10 9 8 7 6 5 4 3 2 1

TORO

Crossed lives of man and bull

Photography
Ramón Masats

Text
Joaquín Vidal

KÖNEMANN

The bulls of Guisando, one of the earliest representations of *Bos taurus*.

If painting and poetry can be said to pay homage to the culture of bullfighting, as it deserves, the Spanish language itself cannot be far behind, since Spanish speakers have filled and enriched their language with metaphorical expressions that sometimes come directly from the world of bullfighting. A symbiosis between words and art has developed, with certain expressions used in everyday speech conjuring up the beauty and danger of bullfighting. Metaphors are born of the concrete images of the art.

Joaquín Vidal shows how the language of everyday speech in Spain is enriched by concepts that come straight from the idiom of bullfighting. Often, before embarking on an important or audacious venture, one speaks of the task in hand as having *trapio*— "power," in the language of bullfighting; of *acosos y derribos*—"pursuing and bringing down," referring to the process by which the fighting spirit of young bulls is tested by men on horseback; of having good *casta* (breeding), of being alert and quick off the mark; and of sometimes being *al quite* (ready to help, or, in bullfighting terms, on hand to draw the bull away).

Much more than simply a photographer, and through the medium that he knows best, Ramón Masats takes us from *Bos taurus primigenius* of ancient Iberia to the pageantry of masterly *verónicas* (passes with the cape), a term itself imbued with highly religious meaning.

Through the medium of words and photographs, this book is a tribute to the art and culture of bullfighting. Words become pictures; the photographs themselves sometimes speak volumes thanks to the magic and color of the *fiesta*, the fighting spirit of its protagonist—the bull—and the skill, elegance, and inspiration of the bullfighters.

Bullfighting comes alive even for those uninitiated in this controversial aspect of Spanish culture. A young boy and a young bull: their crossed paths present, in vibrant words and images, a new perspective on this time-honored tradition.

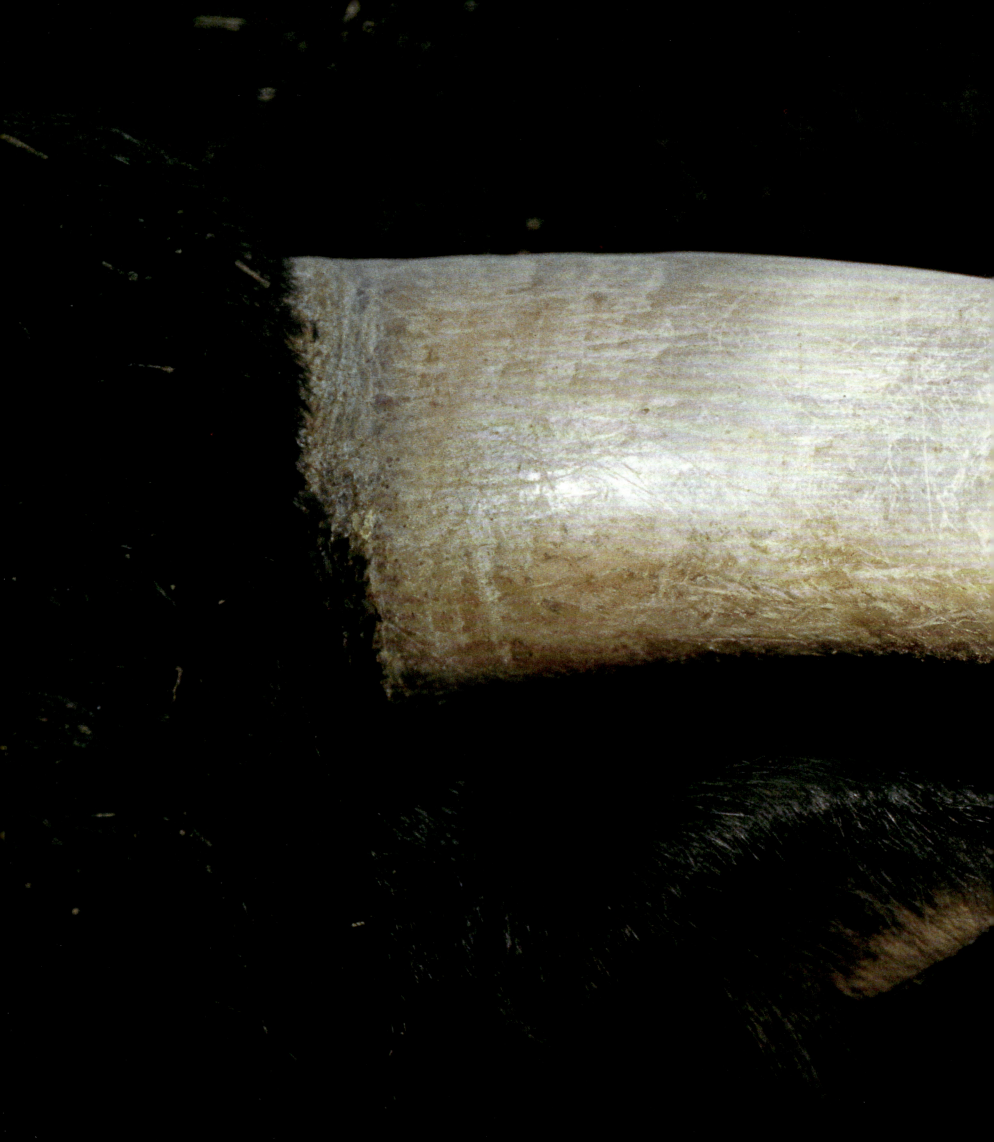

12 to 15. In its natural habitat the fighting bull leads a peaceable existence;
it becomes watchful only when strangers come into view.

16, 17. Bull calves are as playful as any young animals,
and show their fighting spirit very soon after their birth.

18 to 24. Climate affects the development and temperament of the animals and also dictates the appropriate times for branding and carrying out other tasks on the ranch.

25. The late Eduardo Miura, owner of the legendary ranch that bears his name.

26, 27. The *tienta* is the method that stockbreeders use to test the fighting spirit of young bulls, so as to identify those that will perform best in the bullring.

28, 29. The bull, the essential element in the art of bullfighting, is bred for its fighting spirit, which is tested in the *tienta* ring of every ranch.

32 to 34. Pursuing and knocking down young bulls is another way of identifying animals with fighting spirit. This is done by accomplished horsemen wielding goads.

36 to 38. *Banderilleros* perform in the historic bullring at Chinchón. Rafael Peralta (above)
and the Portuguese João Moura (opposite), both masters of bullfighting on horseback,
execute the second phase of the bullfight, in which barbed darts are stuck into the bull's neck.

40, 41. When spring comes, the fields of the ranch
are carpeted with lush grass and wild flowers.

42 to 46. Bulls seem to have a deeply ingrained instinct for fighting. Despite the vigilance
of the stockmen, they sometimes split off from the herd and fight to the death.

48, 49.
A bull shut in the
bullpen and its antithesis:
a bull running free through
the streets takes onlookers
by surprise.

50, 51. Running bulls through the streets in Pamplona,
the most famous bull-running festival in the world.

52, 53. Bull-running is always dramatic and exciting, and can sometimes end in death or injury.

54, 55. The bulls are kept in the corral before their time comes to enter the bullring.

56 to 59.
Sorting animals
before the bullfight.

60 to 63.
The *toril* door leading
from the bull pens
through which the
bull passes when
it enters the ring.

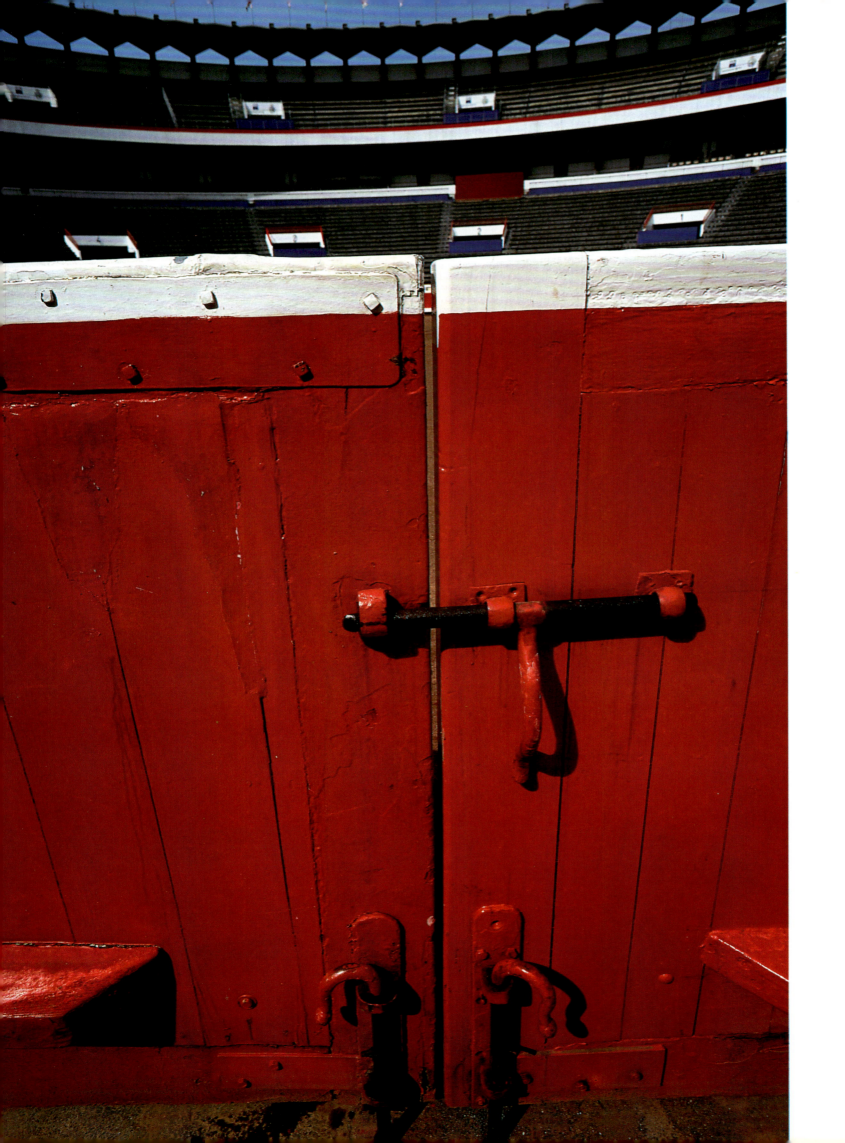

64 to 67. The bullring may be covered or open.
Before a bullfight the ground is smoothed and the lines marked out.

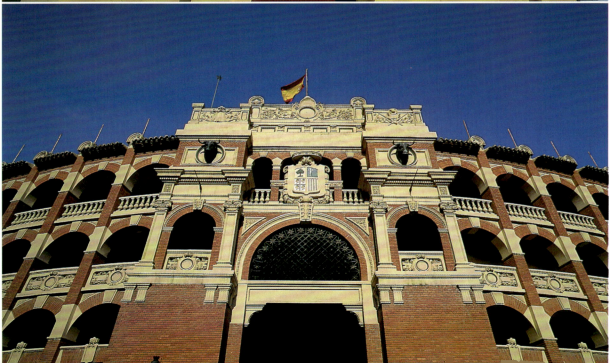

68.
The Puerta del Príncipe at
La Maestranza bullring (top);
the bullring at Albacete (center)
and at Zaragoza (bottom).
69.
The Monumental bullring at
Las Ventas, in Madrid.

70, 71. A bullfighter is dressed for the ring.

72, 73. The matador Víctor Puerto. A matador wears a *traje de luces* ("suit of lights"),
richly embroidered in gold, silver, and silk.

74 to 77. Fiesta in Segovia; festival in San Isidro; ancient stones in the bullring at Béjar.

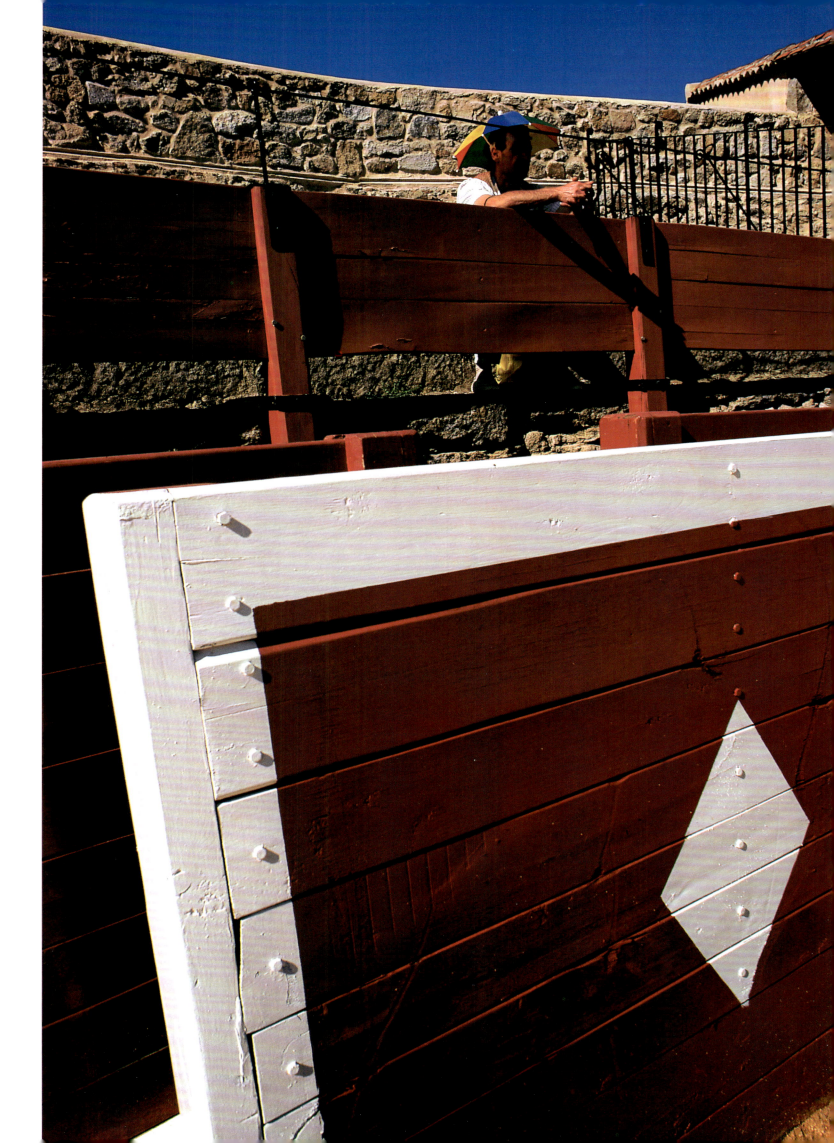

78 to 80. The afición (ardent fans) arrive early in Murcia and Valencia.
In Alicante, a full stadium listens as the band marches out to the sound of the paso doble.

81. The matador Curro Romero, acclaimed in Seville.

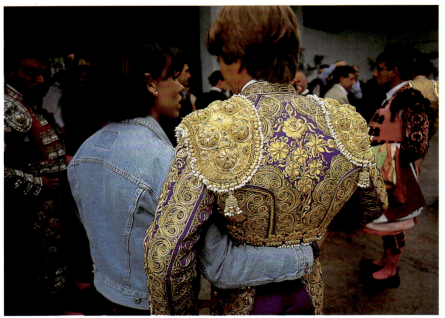

82. The picador wears steel leg armor and his horse protective coverings.
82 (below) and 83. Finery is worn for the opening procession.
84, 85. Rafael de Paula, every inch the bullfighter.

86 to 94. Capes laid out ready for the bullfight. The *cuadrilla*, the team of matador's assistants, enters the bullring at Las Ventas, in Madrid. The *cuadrilla* in the bullring at Ciempozuelos. The afición come armed with cigars, or with sprigs of rosemary to throw at a favorite matador.

96, 97. A bull gallops out of the pen.
Some bullfighters believe that it is unlucky to see the bull enter the ring.

98, 99. Bullfight in Valencia: the bull, entering the ring, faces the matador Enrique Ponce.

100, 101. Fleet of foot, fierce, and fearless, the bull is an animal that commands respect.

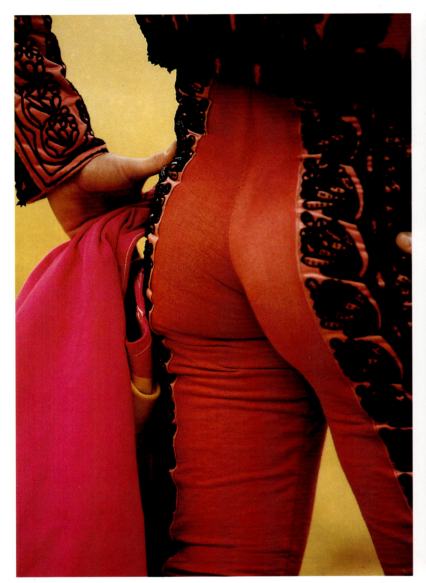

102 to 105. Waiting for the action to start. And then it never stops.

106 to 109. Pageantry in black and gold. Rafael de Paula (opposite) performs the *verónica*, a pass made with feet apart and cape held in both hands.

110 to 113. Opposite: *verónica* or *chicuelina*?
Above: Curro Romero and Rafael de Paula resolve the issue.

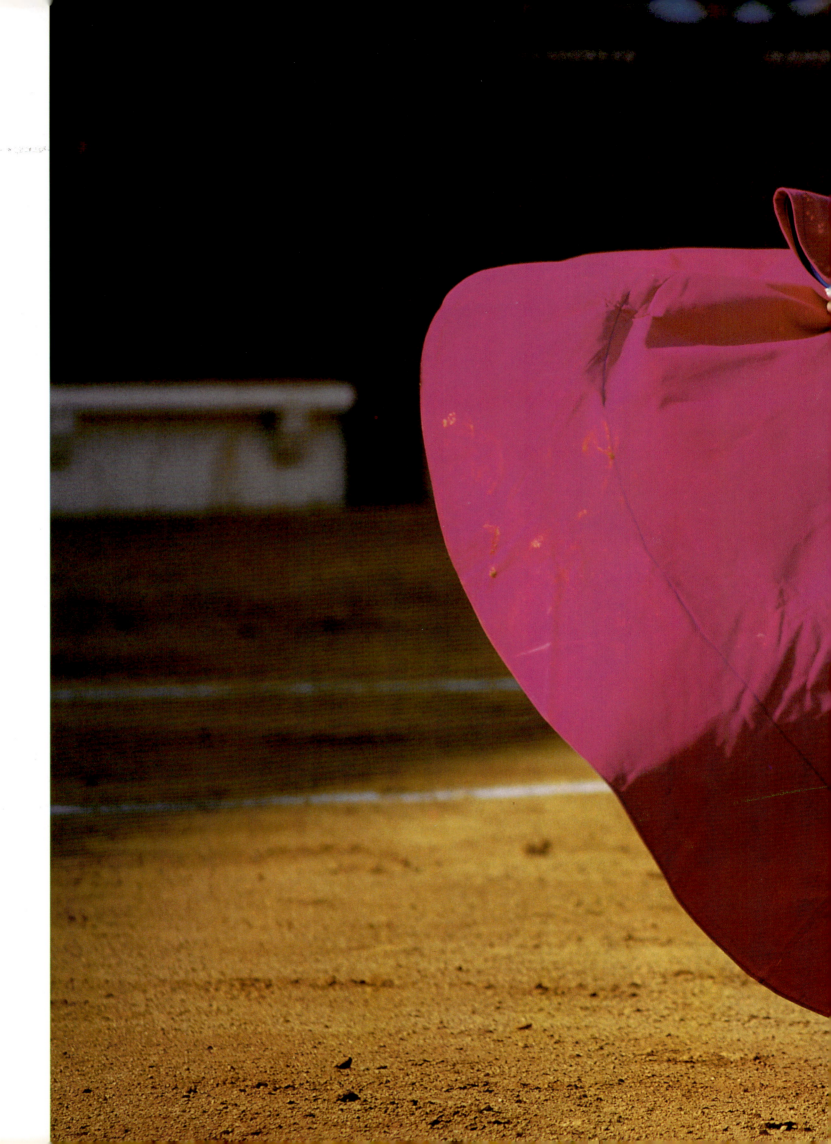

114 to 118. The *delantal*, the *larga*, the *revolera*. Cameras snap at the action.

120 to 126. Aspects of bullfighting: the point of the picador's lance;
an alignment of headwear—the *castoreño*; the picador and his shadow, bravery and power.

128 to 130. The art of planting *banderillas*, demonstrated by Víctor Mendes
and the *banderillero* known as El Formidable.

132, 133. "Brindo por usía" ("I dedicate to your Lordship") is a ritual phrase.
In modern times, bullfighters such as Litri have changed the words to
"Con su permiso" ("By your leave"), except when the king is present,
when custom dictates cheers for his presence and for Spain.

134 to 136. Cristina Sánchez and Luis Francisco Esplá demonstrate
two different ways of beginning a move.

137 to 141. A range of styles: left and above: Manolo Sánchez performing
an *ayudado por bajo,* with the red cape held low;
the *derechazo,* a pass made with the cape in the right hand in the Maestranza, Seville,
with the Giralda, the tower of Seville Cathedral, in the background;
a classic *redondo surcido* demonstrated by Rafael de Paula,
one inspired afternoon in Aranjuez; and Curro Romero, who followed him shortly afterward.

142 to 145. The *derechazo* and the *natural*, a close pass made with the cape in the left hand.
These two regular passes are basic to working with the cape.

146, 147. El Tato tempts fate and escapes by a whisker; the afición breathes again.

148

148, 149. While all eyes are on one matador in the heat of the fight,
another eases the tension of waiting with a cigarette.

150 to 153. *Tremendismo*, reckless behavior with the bull,
is a digression in the art of bullfighting; its most dramatic form is the *pase de pecho*,
in which the matador kneels, his chest level with the bull's horns.

154, 155. The crowd applauds a matador
executing the *pase de pecho* in the style of Belmonte.

156. And for a sudden inspiration, the *afarolado*.

158, 159. An unusual setting: a bullfight in Buitrago.

160, 161. Two classic examples of the *pase de pecho*: to the left and to the right.

162, 163. The bullfighter in daylight and darkness:
the execution of the *manoletina*, in which the cape is held behind the body.

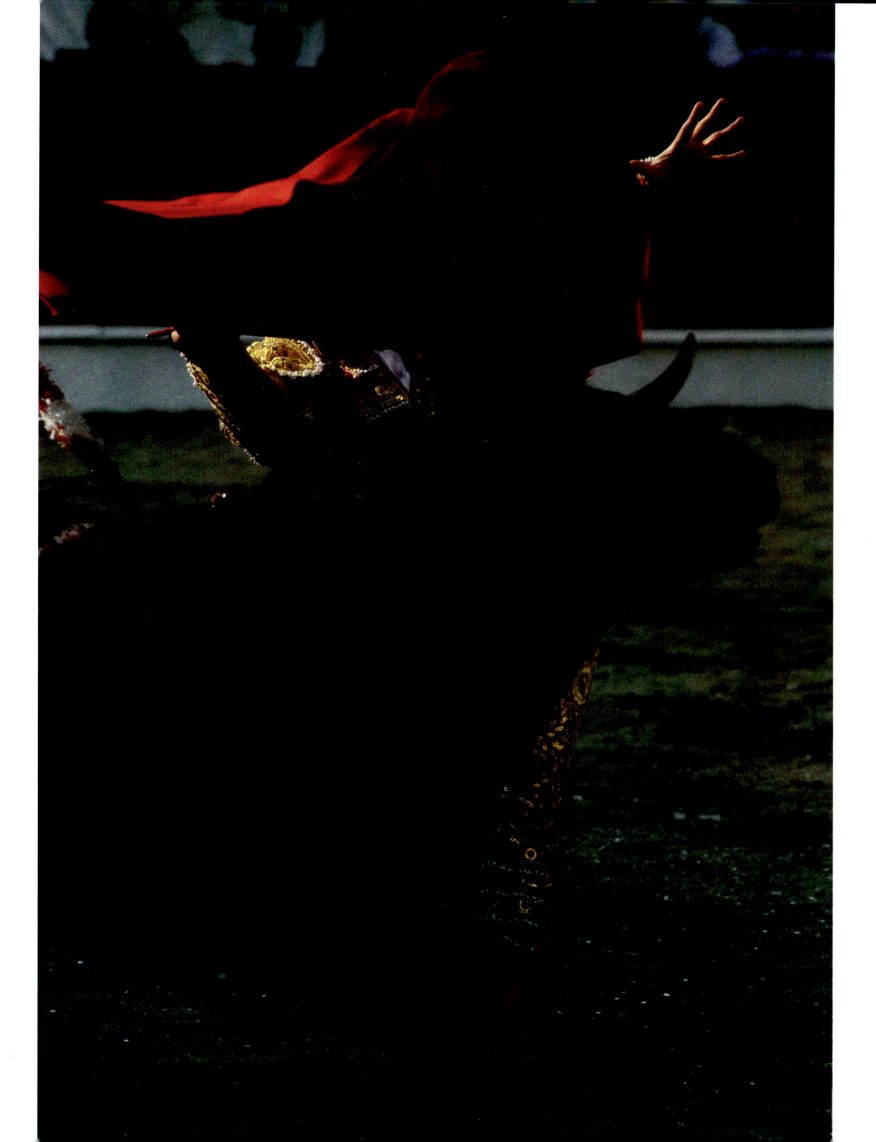

164, 165. Spectacle and spectator.

166, 167. In the crowd, traditional Spanish dress. In the bullring, a matador's silk stockings.

168 to 172. A unique art, daring, fleeting, ephemeral.

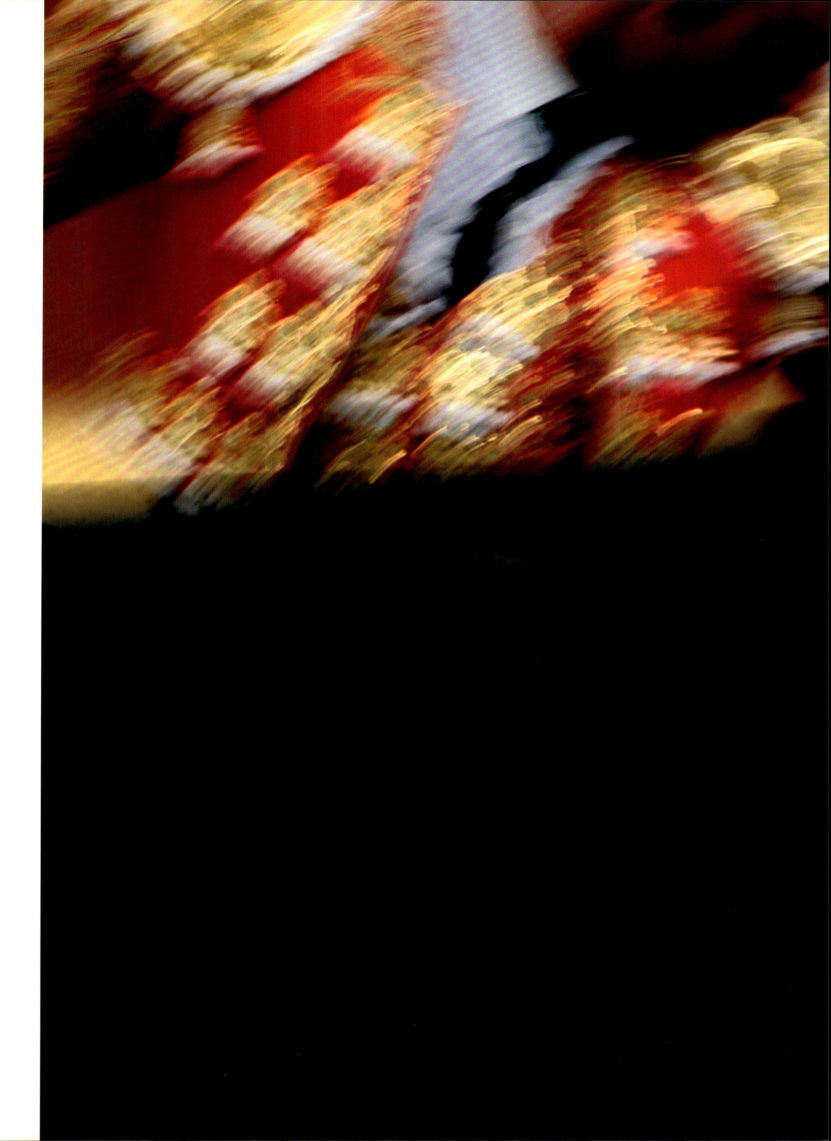

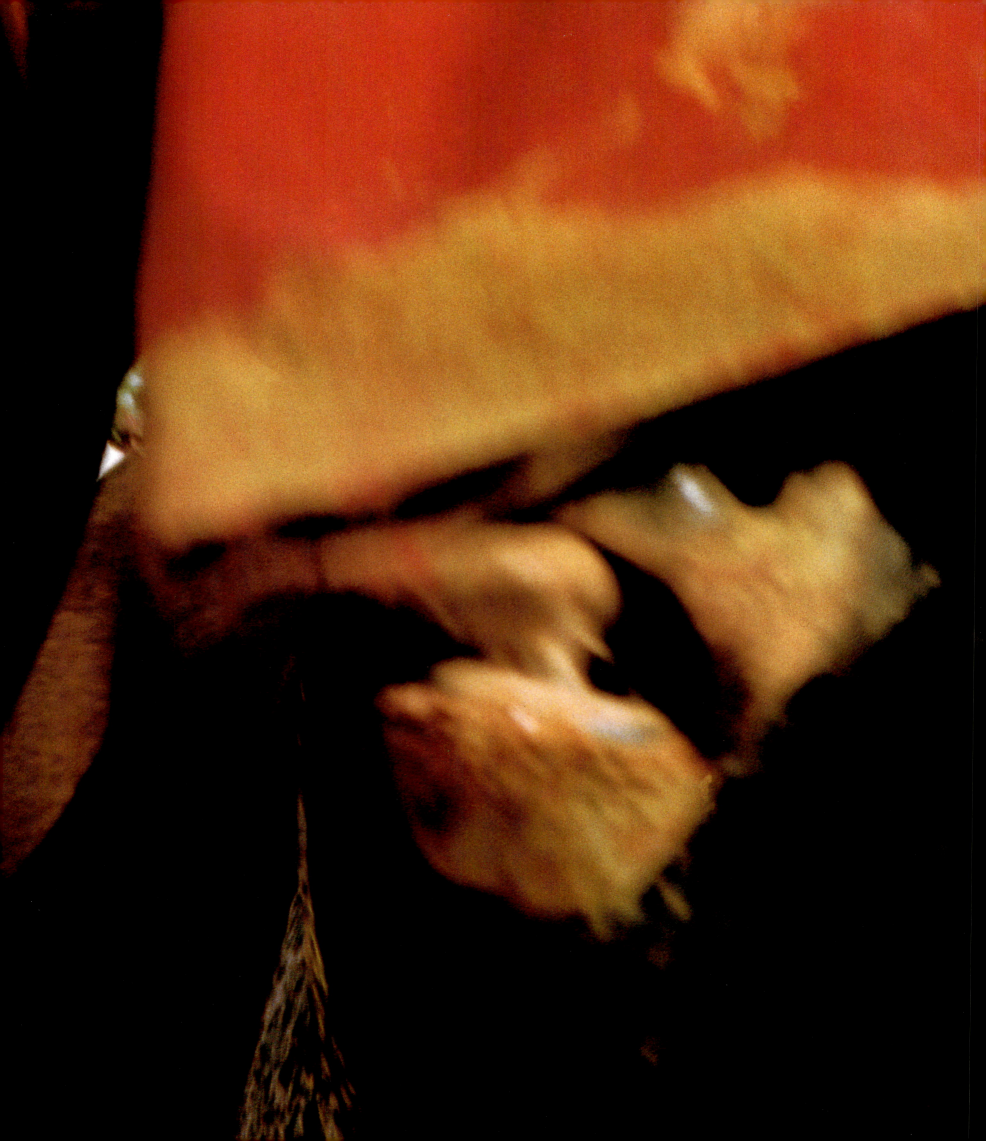

174 to 178.
Sometimes the beauty of
bullfighting turns ugly,
as the danger inherent
in the art materializes in
the form of a goring.

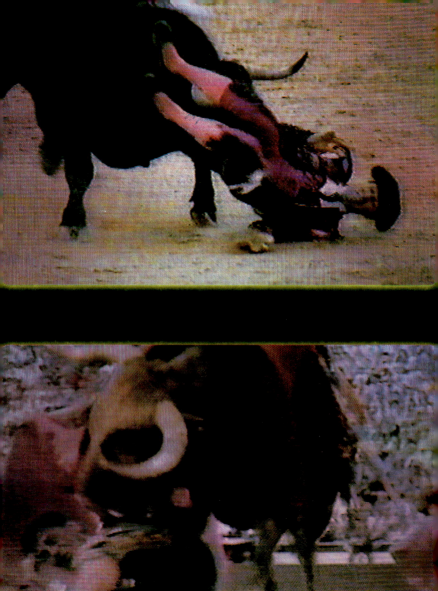

180. In the heat of the fight.

181. Every afternoon, bullfighters' assistants make up the *muletas*.
The *muleta*, a red cape attached to a stick, is an essential piece of equipment in the bullring.

183 to 187. The *suerte suprema*, the final phase of the bullfight.

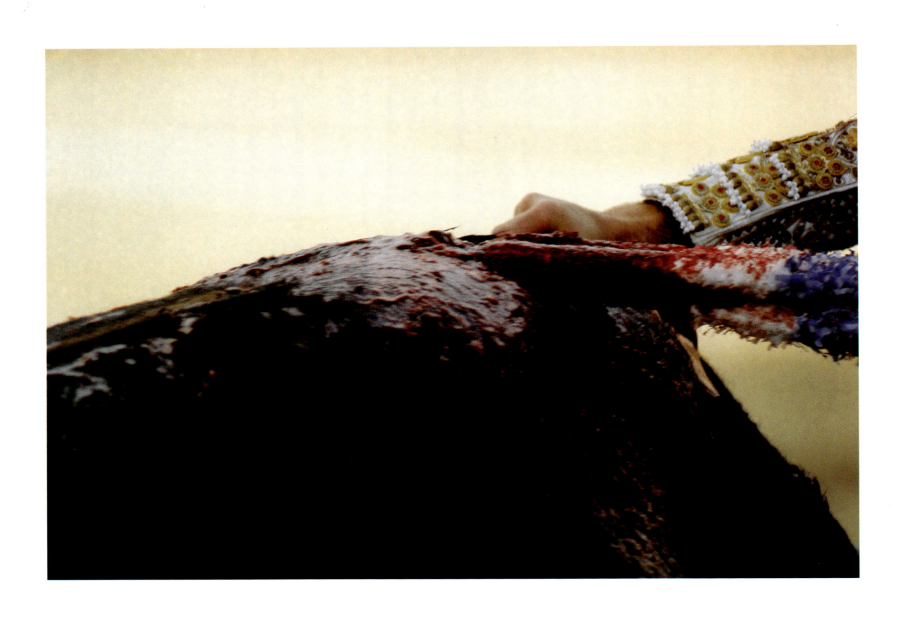

188, 189. The *volapié*, the running sword thrust.

190, 191. The bull staggers, wounded by the thrust of the sword.

192 to 196. Crowds wave handkerchiefs to cheer the matador.
When the bull collapses, the fight is over. All the tension that has built up
dissolves in an explosion of joy, triumph, and euphoria in the moment of glory.

200 to 204.
Victory in the bullring brings glory to the matador. The death of the bullfighter means reaching the heights of glory. The mortal remains of El Yiyo, who was gored in the heart, were accorded a rousing ovation as they were ceremoniously paraded round the bullring at Las Ventas, in Madrid. Joselito el Gallo, the greatest bullfighter of all time, rests in an impressive mausoleum in Seville, built by Mariano Benlliure.

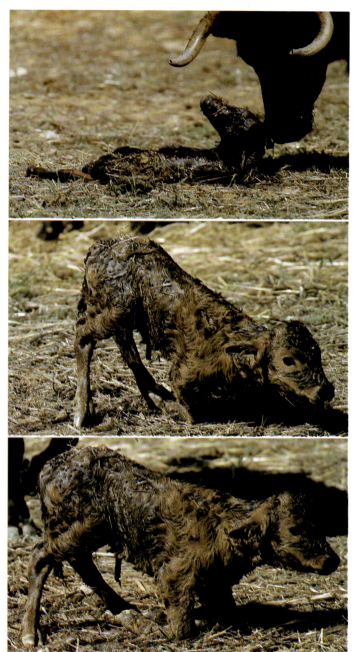

207 to 209. The cow gives birth alone in a secluded part of the ranch.
No sooner has the newborn calf fallen to the ground than it staggers
to its feet and takes its first drink of milk from its mother.
Already it is showing signs of charging, a sure indication of its fighting spirit.

210 to 213.
The art of bullfighting is taught with the aid of a
carretón, a pair of horns mounted on a wheel.
Aspiring bullfighters attend schools of bullfighting
from a very early age. These youngsters have
everything to learn, as does the young bull.

TORO

The bull, *Bos taurus primigenius*, wandered freely beneath the trees of early Iberia. It was master of the land, and Iberian man wanted a toehold there. This conflict probably lies at the remote heart of a complex confrontation that is today known as bullfighting and which developed to the status of the fiesta.

Bos taurus primigenius, the type of bull today used in bullfighting, is present in all cultures. It is, however, most prominent in Mediterranean cultures, and this has been the departure point for scholars seeking to identify the early origins of the modern cult of bullfighting, citing the palace at Knossos, in Crete, and certain initiation and fertility rites. But all of this is surely no more than a fanciful yarn that makes good reading.

The fighting bull, a fearsome, aggressive, wild, and imposing creature, when in its natural habitat, is capable of standing its ground. Human beings, who arrived to challenge the bull's sovereignty, learnt to do battle with its horns. Precisely how this first encounter evolved over the long time span between these remote times and the final years of the second millennium can never be known; it is an encounter that developed into royal tournaments in which the nobility engaged in displays of valor and horsemanship before the court and the king, calling for bulls to be released for the spectacle, and executing dangerous moves while pursuing the beasts with lances and finally killing them.

All we know for certain is how things did turn out. The ordinary populace soon joined in the spectacle, in a servile capacity that matched their social standing, for the nobility needed their help in reducing the dangers of bullfighting and, as far as was possible, increasing the beauty of the spectacle. Assistants thus became part of the game, being brought in to perform what are known today as *quites* (moves to draw the bull away from a bullfighter in trouble); they would divert the bull's attention if it charged dangerously and, being on foot, could help the horseman out in a variety of ways, running around the bull, focusing it, and allowing it to chase them, even if they ended up being tossed in the air on the bull's horns, lucky to escape with their lives.

This, however, marked the beginning of the end of such displays on the part of the nobility, played out before the king and his court. They, along with the ordinary people who were allowed to watch these contests, found it much more interesting and exciting to watch the fleet-footed exploits of the assistants than the highfalutin displays of the gentlemen on horseback.

From then on, the confrontation between man and bull would be on foot, using capes. It was to lead to the institution of bullfighting, which in turn became a great public spectacle, and was to inspire a whole culture that was to become very deep-rooted in the Iberian peninsula.

That is not to say that bullfighting on horseback has disappeared for good, for in the second half of the 20th century it has undergone a revival that would have been unimaginable in previous centuries. Cañero and Simao da Veiga, bullfighters in the days before the Spanish Civil War, had a decisive influence on the increased popularity of bullfighting on horseback, which was perfected and given prestige first by Álvaro Domecq y Díaz and later by Ángel Peralta. New exponents came along transforming the mounted bullfight into a brilliant display of horsemanship. Lupi, the Portuguese bullfighter, brought to the art a consummate technique and introduced new passes, establishing a school of mounted bullfighting whose greatest exponent is João Moura. By the 1970s and 1980s an outstanding team of mounted bullfighters had turned the genre into pure showmanship.

This obviously is another genre of bullfighting, which although it never detracted from bullfighting on foot (referred to as ordinary bullfighting), also developed with remarkable force right from the start. The concerted decision of those who took part in what was already beginning to be known as bullfighting was nothing short of a stroke of genius—to mount a spectacle in which the ferocity of the bull was matched to the skill of the bullfighters.

Those first bullfighters were simple country people, and probably illiterate, and yet they were capable of drawing up a set of rules that matched up to the essential characteristics of the bull and the various ways it can behave, with the appropriate moves to dominate it. The spectacle developed in such a way as to allow the bull to display all his power and fighting spirit. Thus the bull itself became the focus of the spectacle. Breeders of fighting bulls were then able to gauge the qualities of each, which would be useful to them in breeding and selecting further animals.

From this juncture there developed the *tercios*, each of the three main stages of the bullfight. The first was carried out by the picador, a man mounted on horseback and carrying a lance, whose task it would be to provoke the bull's ferocity and fighting spirit; the next was carried out by the *banderilleros*, who would revive the bull's ire by sticking barbed darts into its neck; the third, performed by the matador, the star of the show, would lead to the death of the bull. The whole performance would be accompanied by an endless series of moves with the cape, which the matador would incorporate to embellish the ever-dangerous, exciting, and beautiful spectacle with an elaborate display of his bravery, skill, and mastery.

These stages were not carried out in random fashion. If they were in the early days, it was not long before the techniques of jabbing, planting the darts, stabbing, and killing the bull became clearly defined, as experience dictated how everything should be done. When a bull charges, it lowers it head, and this became the determining factor in the configuration of all the rules. The fathers of bullfighting defined the basic rules, none of which was arbitrary or dogmatic—all were based on close observation of the behavior and actions of bulls.

A fighting bull will rise to the challenge of punishment.

A fine fighting bull will charge with a vengeance, well-focused on the cape; this is what in time came to be called a bull's nobility.

A bull must show his fighting spirit when lanced in the first stage of the fight.

A bull will not be thought to have fighting spirit if it does not attack when it is lanced, turning on the source of the punishment, unless it then shows sustained nobility in the moves made with the cape.

Stockbreeders always bore these factors in mind when they came to select cows and stud bulls for breeding. If a group of bulls from a certain herd did not show sufficient fighting spirit when put to the test by lancing, that was a sure sign that their selection had been unsuccessful.

Many modern stockbreeders—and modern times, in bullfighting terms, go back as far as 50 years—have got this the wrong way round, however. They often belittle the importance of testing a bull with lances, giving preeminence to the animal's nobility in moves with the cape; this is the reason behind their breeding docile bulls.

In those 50 years of modernity many ranches that were highly favored by bullfighters for the mild nobility of their animals fell into a state of decay, and some of them were obliged to close down completely. This was precisely because their stock was bred with the above mentioned characteristics in mind and with scant regard for inherent fighting spirit, which became obvious when the bull was tested with the lance.

But it was the use of the lance on which the fathers of bullfighting based the structure of the fight. The basic stage was the *suerte de varas* (in which the picador weakens the bull with his lance), which would produce the best and most exciting moves of the show. The bull was the focus of attention, his bravery and power apparent. Immediately, he shared the limelight with the picador, who displayed his skill with the implement. The bull was not lanced cruelly and endlessly, as usually happens today, but briefly and lightly, as the bullfighters on the ground prepared to execute *quites* to divert the bull's attention, using a variety of elegant moves, and rivaling one another in the recognition of their skill. The entire period of confrontation, which offered opportunities for displays of expertise, artfulness, charm, and courage—that could at times reach the point of recklessness—was charged with excitement.

The bugle sounded to mark the end of that phase of the bullfight, when the spectacle of the bull displaying every ounce of his power and ferocity had been played out; the spectacle of the picador, adept and daring, often on the receiving end of thumps from the bull and even fractures and goring; the spectacle of the matadors, with their art, their pride, and their daring; of the assistants, who have a perfect mastery of their role. Two more phases of the fight are still to be played out and the art of bullfighting has yet to reveal all its grandeur.

The nobility of bullfighting is unimaginable without the bull and without the bullfighter who dares to confront the beast and who knows how to dominate it. The bull, *Bos taurus primigenius*, that fearsome, imposing, and proud creature, who arrogantly took over the leafy groves of the Iberian peninsula, inspired an art comprised of genius and bravery that we today call the fiesta, and which has grown into the greatest spectacle in the world.

There are bulls that look at their reflection in the water.

"The bull is admiring himself … in the mirror of the river," goes the popular folk song about the bull who falls in love with the moon. It is true of most animals, including the fighting bull. However, while some bulls have all day to look at their reflection in streams running through their pastures, others hardly avail themselves for one moment of this opportunity.

Water, though, is certainly a key factor in the location of a ranch. Ideally, a ranch should have a river running through it, or there should be a lake on the land. These water sources are as likely to be found in marshy areas as they are on what appears to be arid land (that is, land that is dry and barren for long periods of the year).

Stockbreeders disagree as to the best conditions for rearing fighting bulls. Some favor land that offers plenty of lush grass; others maintain that dry, unirrigated land provides better grazing. This has a direct effect on the bulls' weight and build, which in bullfighting parlance is known as *trapío* (power). It is an important issue, but there are authorities who also consider that the type of feed given to the animals affects their fighting spirit.

The whole matter is wide open to debate. No one has reduced the rearing of bulls to pure science. In any case, any bull that gets as far as the ring will be a perfect specimen; always and without exception his power will be beyond dispute, his strength invincible, his fighting spirit sure and inexhaustible, his nobility consummate. The method used by most stockbreeders must therefore be the best possible and they have as a whole developed a science—perhaps an art—for rearing the fighting bull, which has impressive results.

Cattle farmers of centuries gone by should be recognized as the originators of this science. The bulls that inhabited the woodlands of the Iberian peninsula were herded into farms where people who had earned their trust embarked on the demanding task of breeding offspring with an impressive physique and a spirit that seemed made for bullfighting, as well as a resilience that provided bullfighters with opportunities to display their skills.

It was essential to maintain strong strains. These strains differed according to area and origin. The strain is the fighting bull's pedigree. In everyday speech, "strain" (*casta*) is referred to as "race," and the meaning is understood, although it would be better if the latter term were dropped since it causes confusion between the species itself and its physical and mental makeup. "Race" is the zoological term referring to the bull; "strain" refers to the characteristics of its physical and mental makeup. A thoroughbred bull can be fierce or docile, noble or wild, given to trusting docility or imbued with that dangerous sense that was once described as *pregonao*. By maintaining strains, stockbreeders of times gone by were bequeathing to their heirs, over centuries and without interruption, cattle with distinctive characteristics that affected their external appearance as much as their internal makeup, their temperament. Some ranches have herds with such distinct personalities that one only has to set eyes on one of their bulls to know where it comes from.

The most distinctive, direct, and immediate indication of strain is the color of a bull's coat. While this is an outward indicator, it does not tell the whole story, however. The color of the coat must the viewed along with the shape of the bull's horns, which is also an indication of its ranch of origin; different ranches breed bulls that tend to have horns that point forward, downward, straight out, and so on. Both the color of the coat and the shape of the horns should be viewed, in turn, with the animals' build. On some ranches a preference is given to bulls that stand tall and broad, that are medium-sized, or that have an elongated body, with long legs, broad shoulders, a deep chest, and so on.

The fathers of bullfighting had a name for every type of bull, shape of horns, and color or coat, differentiating them down to the smallest detail. And they compiled a brilliant and imaginative catalog listing all the movements and states of the bull during the fight and the multiplicity of moves that took place during its course. This produced a very rich vocabulary, a specific language that was quite distinct from ordinary speech. The Spanish language now contains a great many words and figures of speech that originate from bullfighting.

An unfortunate development, though, as far as the special nature of the fiesta is concerned, is that today things are going the other way. Many people in the bullfighting world use colloquial speech in the context of the display, speaking in an unnecessarily roundabout or metaphorical way that has nothing to do with bullfighting, and promoting a fashion for a way of speaking that is unimaginative, impersonal, ordinary, and ugly; examples include such expressions as the bull "that serves" or "that lets himself be taken," or figures of speech referring to bulls as "cows."

Such abuse of the classic language of bullfighting is causing its specialist vocabulary to be corrupted, relegating it to obscurity and hastening its disappearance. This may not be an exaggeration since, to take the matter a step further, the net result is that the vocabulary of this very new speech is not only alien but runs contrary to the true essence of bullfighting.

The beauty of the bull in open ground should be carried through to the spectacle of the bullfight, and so it was over the centuries until modern times. That statement should be qualified, though. The bullfighting fiesta is neither ancient nor modern. It came into being and remained in a continual state of evolution without any particular period standing out. Problems arose when it was suggested that the anachronistic concepts in the art of bullfighting should be reviewed and adjusted to fit in with the tastes of the modern times in which we live. Needless to say, the proposition had its own agenda. The bull with its characteristic class, power, and strength of spirit was to be done away with, substituted by the feeble and bewildered animal that is now seen all too often in the bullring; likewise the bullfight, which was a display of dominance, a process of closing in on the bull with a series of smoothly executed passes, was to be substituted by a performance made up of a series of disconnected, distant, and repetitive passes.

Cattle farmers of the past who preserved strains and passed them down unadulterated to later generations, together with the bull in all his majesty, power, belligerence, do not deserve such lack of respect from their successors. Neither should the beautiful fiesta, for which these cattle farmers bred the bulls—the essential element of the fiesta—be condemned to such a fate.

The bull in all its majesty…

The bull in its natural habitat is a peaceable creature grazing on pastureland as long as it is hungry and spending the rest of the time taking a siesta.

Bulls move slowly around a ranch and sometimes cluster together in groups under clumps of trees. It is not unusual for one of their number to break away or move off to brood over who knows what frustrations in the shade of a distant copse. Stockmen are alert to the animals' movements and they often have to gallop off in search of a stray animal. It is not difficult to find them: the stockmen have an intimate knowledge of every individual on the ranch. Having known them since birth and watched them mature they know their habits and preferences.

For reasons that cannot easily be explained in human terms, some bulls fight each other. For our entertainment, writers have penned love stories and tales of jealousy, with vengeance cruelly wreaked; for all that they make good reading, these stories are surely not based on fact, since bulls that are destined for the ring do not father calves and are not even put with cows.

Asserting claims over territory, however, can lead to conflict, and arguments over food in a trough also appear to cause skirmishes. But the reason why a whole herd will take against one of its members remains a complete mystery.

We were on a visit to a well-known ranch located in the steep escarpments of the Sierra Morena and in the course of touring around it, we came to a spot where there were mature young bulls, all of them four-year-olds who in a few months' time would be taken to different bullrings. The stockbreeder was pointing out each

bull in turn, telling us where he was to fight, when he was horrified to see that one bull was bleeding from around the eye.

The wound did not look as if it had been made by a horn. Perhaps it had been caused by a stumble or an accidental knock against some boulder in the stony terrain. Whatever the cause, the wound needed attention and the stockbreeder ordered one of his stockmen to go back to the main building and fetch a tranquilizer gun. As we waited we continued our close inspection of each animal in the herd, which went on grazing peacefully. The mastiffs romped about in and out of the herd without the cattle paying any attention, and not even a fit of barking from the most mischievous and frolicsome of the dogs upset them.

At last the stockman returned with the gun and some antiseptic cream, which he handed to the stockbreeder. The stockman loaded the gun with a tranquilizing dart, raised it to his shoulder, and fired at the wounded bull. At first nothing happened: all the animals went on grazing, oblivious to the activity surrounding them. But soon the tranquilizer began to take effect. The bull started to tremble, took a few unsteady paces, and stumbled. Just then, noticing that the bull was about to collapse, the rest of the herd turned on him furiously, butting him with their horns with the obvious intention of toppling him and even killing him.

The attack that had been launched on the bull was really alarming. To break up the brawl the cowherds galloped round the cattle, shouting and hurling stones;

by this time the mastiffs were barking menacingly, jumping up at the bulls to try to sink their teeth into them; the car drivers sounded their horns; everyone was shouting at the tops of their voices to intimidate the aggressors. After a while the bulls dashed off to a nearby hill, in an ill-tempered stampede.

No one who had witnessed the scene could explain why the bulls had turned on one of their number who was obviously in a vulnerable condition. Perhaps the bull had been the tough guy in the herd—even though none of the stockmen remembered him as being so—and his companions had seen their chance for revenge. Perhaps the wound to the eye was the result of an unresolved conflict and the bulls took the opportunity of a replay. Or perhaps it is that the bull in its natural habitat is neither as peaceable nor as noble as it appears, and if certain individuals command respect it is because they lay down the law through force and none of them are sure where they stand in the event of an argument.

The tranquilizer had had the desired effect and the bull fell to the ground, although he was not completely unconscious. He was sitting up and, assisted by the stockmen, the stockbreeder himself made haste to treat the wound by applying the cream with the dexterity of an experienced physician. Meanwhile, we visitors heaped on the dejected bull the bold insults and humiliations that we had seen perpetrated by the masters of brinkmanship at prestigious bullfights. One member of the staff was really daring, grabbing both horns in his hands in the manner of El Cordobés, standing astride its shoulders like Spartacus, or using the horns like a telephone—an old trick of Carlos Arruza's.

The stockbreeder and his staff enjoyed the joke immensely, but it was over quickly because the bull's expression, was giving cause for alarm. Its face did not convey nobility so much as malevolence at that point. It was a fierce, malign, really threatening expression. Of course, it may well have been that my taunts infuriated him and that he was longing to attack me, cursing the moment when a man on a horse took a shot at him and laid him low for a few moments. But this again is pure fantasy. The bull is in fact one of the finest animals on this earth, and this is not at odds with the fact that his fierce genetic makeup contains an instinctive fury that is expressed in aggression, destruction, and death.

If nothing is done to upset him, a bull is a really peaceable creature. This is an axiomatic statement in the stockbreeding world, and there is overwhelming proof of its validity. Every day in all the ranches in Spain—more than 1,000 of them—staff on the estates fill feeding troughs with bulls standing in close proximity without anyone being attacked. Many stockmen approach individual animals with more confidence than the bravest matadors in their finest hours, and some even pet the bulls. And so it is: if you don't do anything to upset them, bulls won't do anything either; they will only be thinking of their own priorities, which are eating and sleeping. That's grand; but it is one thing to speak this axiomatic phrase, and quite another to act accordingly.

Back in our offroad vehicle, we were touring a large ranch, this time in Extremadura, and we had already seen the outbuildings, the horses' stables, the loading area, the place where the cows and their calves were kept, without anything untoward occurring, even though the land was muddy and the stockbreeder had to swerve all the time to prevent the vehicle getting stuck.

Luck eventually runs out, however, and as we neared the place where the fighting bulls were kept, a wheel became stuck in the quagmire, and there it stayed, spinning noisily every time the stockbreeder pushed down on the accelerator to free the vehicle. As it became clear that we were trapped, we got out to assess the situation. We decided that, if we put wedges under the wheels, the vehicle would come out of the mire quite easily. The stockbreeder said to me:

"See that pile of logs over there? Well, go and fetch a few." I replied: "I'd better not; the logs are over there and I can see them. But I can also see the bulls, which are over there, the same distance away as the logs, and they might decide to come over too."

"Don't talk such rubbish," he replied. "You know perfectly well that if you don't do anything to upset them, the bulls won't do anything either."

"All right then. You go," I retorted.

So off went the stockbreeder, muttering under his breath.

A stockman who had spotted us in our predicament from some distance away rode over to the woodpile that the stockbreeder had pointed out, collected some logs, came over to us, and helped position them in a wedge shape. He waited until the vehicle was driven free of the mire and waved us goodbye. The horse also bade us farewell, endorsing the courtesy with a loud whinny. What he was probably saying was "Bunch of greenhorns!" Anything is possible.

The selection of bulls is a rigorous process in which the characteristics of their strain is a key criterion. The crucial test is the *tienta*, the trial to test the fighting spirit of young bulls.

Centuries of experience have shown that the best, perhaps the only, way of testing the fighting spirit of these animals is by seeing how they react to punishment. This is done with the *puya*, the point of the picador's lance, and the moves are practically the same as those in the first phase of a bullfight.

The *tienta* usually takes place in an enclosed bullring, although some stockbreeders prefer to use open ground. They have their reasons: in an enclosed space the bull's scope for running away is limited by the encircling enclosure and, since the picador is always close by, the bull may turn to attack more out of a defensive instinct than out of true fighting spirit. In open ground, by contrast, the bull has the option of running away as far he likes, even seeking refuge among trees; if he reacts by charging, this is an indicator of his fighting spirit.

But the argument works the other way as well. A bull that turns to charge in open ground may also do so for defensive reasons. On yet another view, an enclosed space allows the bull to demonstrate *querencia*, seeking security by returning to the same spot, which is seen to indicate docility.

On a few ranches, the old style of *tienta* is still used for pursuing and bringing down bulls; *garrochas* rather than *puyas* are used and the *tienta* is carried out on open ground by two skilled horsemen. This technique is very suitable for these animals, since they appear not to retain bad memories of the experience. The animal, normally three years of age, is released, pursued, and made to lose its balance by poking it in the ribs with the point of the *garrocha*. Its fighting spirit is then judged by its reactions—whether it turns to confront the horsemen or shies away from them, whether it gets up immediately or lies down defeated, whether it attacks or turns tail.

The many ways in which the *tienta* has been conducted are extremely interesting, displaying an imaginative approach, dedication to bullfighting and the love of the stockbreeders toward their herds. Before the development of the modern *tienta*, some extremely basic devices were used; one method involved placing a mannequin in the center of the enclosure, releasing the animal, and watching it charge. The mannequin stood on a kind of rocker that enabled it to swing back and forth as it was hit by the bull. The call was similar to the lure call used by hunters to attract the wood pigeon since ancient times. Very often, the mannequin fell to pieces or flopped to the ground, and if the animal "despatched" it with a goring, the whole procedure would be judged a success.

This was not a bad way of carrying out a *tienta*; it is known, however, that bulls which "gore" inanimate objects are often not those most suited to the bullring. They can sometimes be the most docile. Many bulls only become more daring when they see the bullfighter defenseless on the ground, and then work off their anger by goring him without mercy. In the days before mannequins were used, a basket was placed in the center of the enclosure and the test lay in seeing how aggressively the bull attacked it. When new methods came into use, this was dropped, although there are those with years of experience who still claim that it must be a valid method, having been used for so many centuries.

The *tienta* carried out in an enclosed space is a serious and rigorous exercise, sometimes misinterpreted or misreported by casual observers. Days that are devoted to *tientas* are important times on a ranch. Bullfighters arrive to watch the proceedings; the stockbreeder courts them for their friendship and also perhaps for their professional engagements; some use the occasion as a public relations exercise and to cement deals with the bullfighting world. On such occasions it is almost like fiesta time on the ranch, although this in no way interferes with the importance of the real task in hand.

The downside to such occasions is the presence among the guests of aficionados who strut around full of airs and graces. For them, stockbreeders have suitable young bulls that allow them to show off without danger. However, some stockbreeders are reputed to smuggle in young bulls that are known to be nasty and sometimes the braggarts get their just desserts.

The guest who has delusions of being a bullfighter really just mimics the style of his favorite bullfighter and the young bull usually sends him running for cover. There are, however, those who have learned the basic principles of the art of bullfighting and take the professionals by surprise. Sometimes, albeit rarely, an aficionado may handle a bull better than the matadors who are there to take an active part in the *tienta*, and this can make for embarrassing situations.

Whatever the case, fighting a young bull one day at a *tienta* is a world away from tackling a feisty bull and emerging victorious. Bullfighting is a very demanding profession that involves much more than performing a few elegantly executed passes. It requires dedication and courage, and this fulltime occupation is a continuous apprenticeship that inevitably involves mishaps, sacrifices, and other unfortunate occurrences. The bullfighter who masterfully fights a challenging bull carries within him an immense wealth of knowledge and experience.

Bullfighters who take part in the *tienta* for female animals need to know the correct technique, understand the different nature of the animals, know how to fight, and exercise strict self-discipline in carrying out the stockbreeder's instructions. As is right, the stockbreeder is in charge of the *tienta*, not because he knows any more about bullfighting than the professionals, but because he has a clear idea of the direction his ranch must take. If the stockbreeder wants his ranch to be a commercial concern—that is, a ranch that breeds relatively quiet bulls, who are not particularly aggressive—it would be absurd to advise him that this approach is in line with rigorous selection and the values of the fiesta, and that he provides matadors with the most docile animals. If his own interest in bullfighting points him in the direction of a ranch that produces top-class animals of indomitable power, he should not be persuaded to weed out strong-willed cattle that will charge aggressively again and again.

One by one the animals burst into the *tienta* ring. The bullfighter lines them up at the correct distance and down comes the *puya*; if the animal recoils, fights free, moves backward, or jerks away when it feels the blow, these are signs of docility. A reputable, scrupulous stockbreeder will immediately reject the animal.

There are, however, quite a few stockbreeders today who, although they are aware of these considerations, are not prepared to reject such an animal and will ask the bullfighter to show it the red cape to see what happens. With the red cape there is no punishment and what often happens is that the beast charges convincingly; at the same time it is easily provoked and slow to return to the attack, and this unchallenging behavior allows the bullfighter to take his time in performing all manner of calmly and elegantly executed moves.

The unscrupulous stockbreeder is impressed by the animal's performance. Far from sending it to the slaughterhouse, he claims that it is an excellent beast; when it reaches maturity he will make it the stud bull. In the view of other more reputable stockbreeders, more experienced professionals, and knowledgeable aficionados, this is a mistake; they believe that by selecting animals by these criteria he will quickly bring his ranch into disrepute. Other colleagues, professionals and aficionados alike, may back his decision and congratulate him because this is the kind of bull they consider ideal for the fiesta. And so it goes.

The way in which the animal performs during its *tienta* is recorded by the stockbreeder in the ranch record books. These books record the entire history of the ranch, containing a record of every animal born there, with its number, its name, and its lineage, its strength, and the color of its coat; when it was branded and when it was put through the *tienta*, and the second *tienta*; what it was put through and how it performed. If the bull made it to the bullring, the record gives details of the fight that it put up in each phase, who the matador was, and how its performance was judged.

A ranch's record books make fascinating reading because they reveal an important aspect of the history of bullfighting from a point of view that is very different from that of the aficionado or the spectator. They throw light on the selection criteria that explain the relevant characteristics of their herds.

The ranch record books show whether successive ranch-owners used the same criteria for selecting animals from the ranch's beginnings up to the present day or whether they tried certain variations. While the former case is rare, the latter is very common. A change in ownership, especially if the ranch is purchased rather than passed down, does not necessarily mean a change in the way the *tienta* is carried out but it is likely that a new stud bull will be brought in, or that cows with a special lineage will be introduced, and this will alter the bloodlines. Alternatively, the entire breeding stock will be removed and a fresh start made; then, all that remains is the name, the *señal*, the *divisa*, and the brand.

The *señal* is the nick made in the animals' ear with a sharp knife. It may take various forms and is known by several names; if not made by incision it is known as an *orejisana*. The *divisa* are the colors indicating the bull's breeder; these colors, specific to each ranch, are indicated by a rosette pinned to the bull's shoulder when it is released into the bullring. The brand is made with a branding iron when the animal reaches one year of age.

After being selected through a *tienta*, the cows are put to the stud bull, usually in April, when they are in good condition, with glossy coats, and come into season. When the stockbreeder thinks best, and normally on the advice of the ranch manager, cows are selected and corraled with a suitable bull; the bull is then given ample time to cover them. The bull does not mate with every cow, and those that have not been covered get another chance later on. Most of the cows will then be in calf, and will give birth nine months later.

To give birth, the cow needs peace, quiet, and solitude. She will usually seek out some kind of sheltered spot, which can just as easily be a fence on the ranch or a group of trees. For their own personal safety, people are advised never to go anywhere near the cow at this time; this is a critical moment when she will be at her most aggressive and dangerous.

The birth is truly a miracle of nature. Anyone who has had the opportunity of witnessing such an event will not forget the magic of watching the tiny creature come into the world, front feet first and then, pushed along by the shoulders, its little head appears. It falls to the ground and almost immediately begins to thrash about almost as if it were trying to charge. The spindly legs are hardly strong enough to support the newborn calf; it staggers, topples over, gets up again, makes as if to attack, flops back on to the ground. The process is repeated several times as the cow moos softly to it, stroking it with her large soft tongue, and the trembling little body is rewarded with the warm sweetness of its first drink of milk.

One of the most beautiful sights that can ever be seen on a stock farm is a group of cows with their newborn calves by their side. The little ones cavort about all over the place, running between their mothers' stout legs. Fights are always breaking out among the calves; they butt one another but it is never anything more than a game. These romps never last long in any case, because the calves never go for long without rushing back to suckle noisily at their mothers' udders. Like all young animals, human beings included, these suckling calves are always keen to feed and happy to be near their mothers.

At nightfall the cows lie down. Drawn to the welcoming warmth of its mother's body, each calf nestles down besides her and goes peacefully to sleep.

The night brings a covering of dew, and in high-altitude pastures there is even frost. Strange noises probably fill the youngsters with fear. In the first night of their lives they must surely be frightened by the howling of the wind, the creaking of branches, and the hiss of the breeze through long grass. If there are waterfalls nearby, the gushing of water will make the kind of sound that always seems a little alarming in the solitude of open spaces. And bellowing will be heard. In areas where bulls are bred, to listen to the night is to experience a mysterious aspect of nature, an aspect that can never quite be understood.

Inside the farmhouse, logs crackle in the grate, and the stockman and his family are gathered round the wide hearth. If they are entertaining friends, the conversation will turn to bulls and bullfighting. Stories will be told and scraps of news exchanged; there is always some unusual story about bulls, among the gossip about love affairs and tales of revenge. Once they have retired for the night, and sleep comes they will hear the same howling and the same murmurs, and from time to time the terrifying bellowing of a distant, fretting bull.

By morning, the cows are already setting off in search of grazing, followed by their calves. The young bulls and the older cattle are each penned in their own field. Now the cowherds come out to see to the herd. They fill the feeding-troughs, going about their work seemingly without fear of danger, even when the cattle are so near.

Among the cattle there is always one that seems unusually alert, and if he then puts on airs and graces, this is a bad sign. But the cowherd's voice calms him. Cowherds have a special way of speaking, a low musical crooning that cattle seem to understand. The comings and goings of the cowherds and the passivity of the animals—which are bred for their ferocity—make for a surprising feeling of intimacy. It is hard to imagine that this could be shared with strangers.

What I now describe is truly extraordinary, and it is one of my most vivid memories of the frequent visits that I have made to ranches where fighting bulls are bred. I had come, as a journalist, to write a story, and the photographer who was with me was Fernando Botán. He and I had been school friends from an early age, and we had remained close, often sharing a joke.

The stockman was going to drive the two of us around the ranch in a tractor. We were sitting in the back of a low trailer and he was telling us in a loud voice how much of the ranch he was going to show us. I was listening, taking in all I could see and jotting down various facts; Botán was taking photographs. We stopped for a while at the feeding troughs. The stockman and the overseer began to fill the troughs with feed. Botán and I, meanwhile, stayed in the trailer, without moving a muscle; the stud bulls were milling about all around us, too close for comfort, and the last thing we wanted to do was draw attention to ourselves.

Somewhat self-consciously I went on scribbling in my notebook, while Botán shot pictures, taking care not to make a sudden movement. Suddenly, to my consternation, he whispered:

"Stop tickling me."

How could I possibly be tickling him when my hands were on my lap, one holding a pen and the other a notebook? I assumed that he was making one of those little jokes, and although it seemed strange in the extreme, I went back to scribbling in my notebook without saying a word. But Botán said it a second time:

"Stop tickling me, you idiot!"

From the tone of his voice I could tell that he wasn't entirely joking, and this time I asked him whether he was not getting a little flustered.

There was a moment's silence: he was thinking hard. As our eyes met, Botán suddenly realized that it wasn't me who was tickling him. We turned round and our blood froze. The mysterious tickler was a bull. A bull had been attracted by the straw that was hanging out of the back of the trailer and had stuck his head in without meaning to poke anyone in the ribs with his horns.

I called out to the stockman. I called again and he didn't hear me. No one could hear me because the fact was I had no voice. I opened my mouth, I frantically moved my lips, I strained my throat, but my vocal chords were completely frozen. Botán was equally speechless with fear. So we sat there in silence as it sunk in that we faced certain death. To our great good fortune, by pure intuition, the stockman came out: he immediately took in the situation and began to croon "Regurregurregu!" The bull, who understood the language, withdrew his head from the trailer, looked round and set off with a deliberate step.

Many years have passed since that time, and I have never understood why that bull didn't spear us with his horns: he could have done it so easily. Certainly we would not have been worth his while but if we had been Joselito or Belmonte, it might have been a different matter: he would have basked in the glory of it. Even someone wandering about looking for wild asparagus would have been a target— if a bull spots a man picking asparagus anywhere on the ranch, he will stick him in the groin. By contrast, a couple of journalists with a camera and a pen are nobodies; they won't get a bull into the history books and they aren't even worth the time it takes to trample them under foot.

"Regurregurregu" is a magical, almost biblical, word. It has the power to exorcise and contains many different levels of meaning. I heard it again on another stock farm a few years later, and for a particular purpose. It was on Victorio Martín's farm. Again, we were making a tour of the ranch, this time in an offroad vehicle. We reached a clump of trees and the famous breeder stopped the vehicle in a patch of shade. He climbed down and said:

"Get out and we'll go see the stud bulls."

We started to cross the field and he soon stopped and pointed:

"This is the place."

We looked all around and absolutely nothing was in sight. So I said:

"This might be the place but I can't see a single bull, Victorio."

"Wait. Here they come."

As he said this, he cupped his hand to his mouth and called out the magic word over and over again:

"Regurregurregu, regurregurregu!"

When the calling was done he pointed to a nearby hill; we watched and a couple of minutes later the bulls appeared over the brow of the hill. At first just their horns were visible; then gradually their great bodies came into sight as they came closer and closer. Quite calmly, they came right up to us, stopping when Victorio said "So!", or some such command.

Eleven bulls like eleven devils from hell lined up quietly before us less than a stone's throw away and eyed us with curiosity.

"We've never seen such pale-faced humans; they must be English," the bulls seemed to be mooing to one another. "Not only pale-faced but *so* tremulous; at the very least they must be suffering from St Vitus's dance," they added.

They seemed to feel sorry for us, since none of them made as if to charge, which was just as well because where we stood there was no fence or barrier; no wall to leap over, no olive tree to climb, nor hole to dive into.

Of the eleven bulls, ten looked at us in some puzzlement, and one—an impressive-looking specimen with a glossy coat—stood slightly apart, rather suspiciously, because he clearly didn't trust us. This was the famous Belador, whose fighting spirit was such that he was spared at a memorable bullfight at Las Ventas, in Madrid. Recovered from the tremendous thrusts of the picador's lance, Victorio made him a stud bull. The experience taught Belador that white men hit hard, especially if he appears wearing a *castoreño*. He had evidently not forgotten it. Fortunately, neither the photographer, María Jesús Polanco—who was on the point of a nervous collapse—nor I were wearing a *castoreño* that day. Happy coincidence!

To the sound once again of "Regurregurregu!"—chanted at a different pitch—the bulls turned tail and went back from where they came. As they disappeared over the brow of the hill, I turned to the photographer in case she was on the point of fainting; in fact she needed no help at all; she had followed everything with great interest and had even taken some very good photographs. If anyone needed help it was me; I was desperate for reassurance. Try as I might, I couldn't help going over in my mind what could have happened if a bull had gone for us or if Belador had decided to wreak revenge. We would have stood no chance.

The stockbreeder's dictum is that, with bulls, everything goes all right as long as you don't do anything to upset them. But it's on condition that you don't pick asparagus. And that you sing to them: "Regurregurregu!"

Authorities on the art of bullfighting believe that bulls bred specifically for the bullring were first raised on specialist stock farms in the 18th century—or perhaps even in the 17th century. There is, however, insufficient evidence to allow the identification of any physical characteristics that set these breeds apart. From the 18th century, and certainly by the 19th, solid documentation exists concerning the activities of stock farms, covering crossbreeding, bloodlines, buying and selling, number of bullfights, head of cattle, and the role of bullfighters.

Throughout almost the whole of the Iberian peninsula, there were bulls with characteristics, albeit not fully developed, that made them suitable for bullfighting. Authorities agreed that the best bulls came from Andalucía; their power and fighting spirit, strength, and nobility made them best suited to the art of bullfighting.

In the second half of the 18th century, two Andalucian grandees, the Count of Vistahermosa and the landowner Vicente José Vázquez, exerted a major influence on the establishment, and development of these stock farms. Vistahermosa had a great enthusiasm for bulls, and a keen eye, and historians hold that his stockman Curro el Rubio knew the livestock intimately. Whatever the case, it seems certain that the count bought his animals from a stockman from Dos Hermanas called Ribas, experimented with the herd, selected from it judiciously, made the right cross-breedings, and came up with an exceptional breed of bull that was marked by its unflagging fighting spirit. These bulls were black and piebald, and of a very handsome build.

Such was the renown of the count's bulls that other stockbreeders soon wanted to benefit from his bloodlines; they bought cows and bulls from him, and interbred them with their own stock, and a time came when almost every bull that was seen in Iberian bullrings could trace its origins back to Vistahermosa. By the beginning of the 20th century, the name had entered the vocabulary of stockmen; and was bandied about in such remarks as "However you try to breed livestock, it will end up like all the rest: *vistahermosando*."

Vicente José Vázquez bought the best stock in the district: this was Utrera, and the animals were again from the Vistahermosa bloodline. He established another major cattle ranch, which reached great heights in his lifetime and had far-reaching effects later on. He bred bulls that were finer than Vistahermosa's; according to some, they had a certain toughness that made them a challenge. This was why many stockmen who aspired to produce animals that would cause a stir in bullfighting circles harbored a desire to breed from them.

When Vázquez died, in the mid-19th century, his heirs sold much of his livestock to Fernando VII, who ran his own cattle ranch in Aranjuez; this ranch was already breeding fighting bulls in the 18th century, when it was owned by King Philip IV. Having undergone this change of ownership, Vázquez's stock was moved from Seville to Aranjuez; it then consisted of 35 *cuatreños* (cattle nearly four years old), 500 cows, and 100 two-year-old cattle. The ranch was later acquired by the Duke of Veragua; it came to be regarded both for the fighting spirit of the bulls that it bred and for their strong build, set off by the beauty of their coats, which were predominantly black, piebald, white, particolored, or tan.

Although bulls from northern Spain had their own individual characteristics, they were soon crossbred with Andalucian stock and gradually lost their distinctive stamp. Bulls from Jijona, in the province of Ciudad Real, formed a famous bloodline; when crossbred with stock from Colmenares their characteristics became so preponderant that the name *jijón*, referring to their particolored coats, became a word for any type of cattle of this color.

According to historians of the time, bulls from Castile were larger and more impressive than those from Andalucía; they were very tough and hardy enough to flourish on sparse land in cold upland areas; they would charge with a vengeance in the bullring, but their fighting spirit was not guaranteed since they tended to become retiring after the first phase of the fight.

Extremadura, Salamanca, and central Castile, however, became the heartland of bull breeding, with some excellent ranches where stockbreeders improved bloodlines through judicious crossbreeding. By the beginning of the 20th century they had established ranches that bred bulls of a distinctive character and excellent quality, which allowed them to compete openly with Andalucian establishments.

The Navarre strain is one of those jewels of bullfighting whose permanent loss, at least in Spain, is lamented by aficionados. Navarrese bulls are small but extremely fiery. Bullfighters did not like them because, while the animals' small size made them less of a challenge, the difficulties that they presented demanded great effort, and their obstinate valor made the fight a laborious affair. The aggressiveness of Navarrese bulls, tireless in their repeated charges, was sometimes indomitable.

Marginalized by the bullfighting profession, Navarrese bulls eventually died out in Spain. This was not the case in Mexico, where this breed of cattle was exported and where the strain boosted bloodlines of major ranches there. Pre-Civil War matadors who fought bulls from these ranches would often remark that these animals retained the essential characteristics of the Navarrese strain. Present-day Mexican commentators affirm that these characteristics can still be discerned in many Mexican cattle.

It is said nowadays that Spanish ranches no longer breed such fine strains. This raises some serious issues, since most of the blame would seem to fall on the stockbreeders. If such is the case, a reverse process has occurred in the long course of development that stretches from the original strains to the type of bull that emerged in the first decades of the 20th century. From the fierce, wild bull that provoked those early risky encounters developed the well-built, courageous, and energetic creature that was ideal for bullfighting. Now, it seems, the bull has no fire, or at least very little.

To the accusation that Spanish ranches have lost class can be added the charge that bulls reach the bullring carrying excessive weight. When a bull weighing almost 1120 lb comes hurtling into the ring, charges round it, and keels over for a couple of minutes, most experts will say that it weighs too much.

One of the many reasons cited for bulls falling down like this is that they do not take enough exercise. Now, a bull in a fitness center is not something you see everyday. Experts who have explained the methods used by stockbreeders in the past to breed their thoroughbred bulls make no mention whatsoever of bulls being kept fit. To make up for lack of exercise, some stockbreeders, several months before their bulls are due to fight, make them gallop in the fields with the healthy aim of toning them up.

Bulls that take part in the Feria de San Fermín in Pamplona tend not to fall over, and bullfighting experts put this down to the fact that they have been exercised the same morning by being run through the streets.

None of these explanations has a firm basis and I disagree with them. I believe that they do not address the real issue and that they are absurd.

I remain slightly dubious: perhaps the ranches haven't lost class after all. This can be seen from the performance of the bull itself. It's quite true that bulls do fall over; they often keel over as soon as they enter the ring. And yet, their encounter with the picador's lance is similar to the punishment undergone in the *tienta*. If the bull did not have class, it would jump up and down in fright when it felt the branding iron, it would run terrified and would hurtle off blindly. The evolution of stock ranches over the centuries shows that the true and perhaps the only way to measure a bull's fighting spirit is to watch its reactions in the first phase of the bullfight when it is lanced by the picador; and they pass this test with flying colors.

A bull's body weight surely cannot be a determining factor in its propensity for falling over. From the beginnings of bullfighting up to the Spanish Civil War, bulls weighed much more than they do today, and they were not prone to falling over. Indeed, the minimum weight for bulls is actually set at 1015 lb. Under regulations laid down in 1923 and in force up until the Spanish Civil War, the minimum weight was set at around 1200 lb for the season running from October to March, and at 1260 lb for the rest of the year.

Weighing at least 1260 lb and often more than 1330 lb, bulls performed all three phases of the fight without mishap; they received many deep strikes of the picador's lance, they brought down and even killed the odd horse, they would rear up even when stuck with barbed darts; by the third phase the matador would have to whip them from below and beat them about the legs in order to repulse their fierce charges. And though they weighed at least 1260 lb they did not fall over.

The Spanish Civil War disrupted many cattle ranches. In some cases the stock was abandoned to its fate; in others the cattle were literally eaten by starving troops and civilians. After the war there were not enough animals with the right power to satisfy the needs of the many festivities that once again were held all over the country as things returned to normal, so that the authorities tolerated, as a temporary measure, a reduction in the age and weight of the animals. At no other time in the history of bullfighting had such diminutive bulls been seen in the ring. Yet they were not prone to falling over.

These bulls did not do exercise. They continued being raised on the ranches just as they always did, doing what came naturally: eating, drinking, sticking a well-aimed horn into the backside of an asparagus-picker—this was their occupation.

A bull in an exercise gym must be a hilarious sight. I believe that the best exercise that a bull could take would be aerobics.

A stockbreeder of noble descent that I once visited on his ranch in the mountains was at pains to convince me that bulls fall over because they do not take exercise. I replied by reminding him of those bulls that are bred relaxed, dissolute, lax, in warm climates, on extensive prairies carpeted with grass, and they never fall over. But it was in vain. Over the breakfast that we were enjoying in the main house, by the warmth of the fire, the stockbreeder insisted on defending the idea of exercise.

Mid-morning we went out to tour the estate and it was noon when he discovered that a bull was missing. He sounded the alarm. The stockmen scanned the horizon, told the boss that they would launch a search, and set off on foot, on horseback, or in cars. After various sorties along paths and tracks and up on to vantage points, someone spotted the bull quietly grazing in a distant depression in the land. The stockmen rode over to the spot and called the bull back.

We had been watching the whole operation from the comfort of a car, and the stockbreeder lamented:

"It's such bad luck that one of the best bulls, which I was keeping for Madrid, should escape. We'll have to see how this trek home will affect the poor thing. Bulls are used to the peace of the countryside and you just can't go putting them through these ordeals."

I was deep in the pleasures of smoking a cigarette and his words brought on a fit of coughing.

The famous Feria de San Fermín is also known as the Feria del Toro. It is organized by the Casa de Misericordia of Pamplona in aid of its humanitarian activities, and the bull-running is organized by a committee made up of experienced aficionados who are experts in the field. For many years the bulls that were provided for Pamplona's festival were thoroughbred, fiery, and of unimpeachable quality. While most other bullrings were provided with bulls that were in bad physical shape, not a single bull that came into Pamplona's ring fell over. All those involved in bullfighting, from promoters, bullfighters, and managers, to aficionados, agreed on the technical verdict:

"Bulls do not fall over in Pamplona because of being run through the streets that morning. They run from the pens of El Gas to the bullring, and that's good exercise. In other words: when they enter the bullring, they're in fine form."

In recent years, most of the bulls that have appeared in the bullring at Pamplona have not been in good physical shape. They would fall over, like everywhere else. All those involved in bullfighting, from promoters, bullfighters, and managers, to aficionados, agreed on the technical verdict:

"Bulls fall over in Pamplona because of being run through the streets that morning. They are not used to being made to run in such races, especially not at the same time as being surrounded by a huge crowd, and they become stressed."

The first time that I heard this explanation I wasn't even smoking, but I again began to splutter.

Stress is a new factor that has been brought into the argument about why bulls fall over. Bullfighting folk say that they fall over as the result of stress induced by the lances that are stuck into them during the fight. At best they want to give the impression that, throughout the entire history of bullfighting, from its beginnings to ten years ago, bulls did not have lances stuck into them but were pampered.

Bulls—so I believe—do not fall over from lack of class, nor because they are not taking exercise or become stressed. They fall over because they fall over.

Ways of handling bulls, cows, and calves on ranches amount to highly specialized techniques. Stockmen do not need to know Latin or mathematics or sit exams, but they do need the kind of experience that cannot be learnt from books.

Branding bulls is no small task, and neither is leading them wherever they need to go. Herding the bulls is almost always done with the aid of *cabestros*, bullocks used to lead fighting bulls into or out of the ring. Raising these bullocks is another highly specialized aspect of cattle ranches. Some groups of *cabestros* are very highly regarded in the stockbreeding world. Samuel Flores' *cabestros*, distinguished by the color of their coats, are very famous, as are those of Miura.

A stockbreeder who owns a good group of *cabestros* can be proud of the care with which he runs his ranch. The correct way of moving bulls back and forth is with the use of *cabestros*, which are essential to the operation, whether it is a single animal that is being driven or a whole herd. The way that the *cabestros* are deployed might be compared to a battle formation. The leader goes first, followed by two others who walk on either side of the horsemen, and two more bring up the rear, or sometimes just one depending on the usual practice on any particular ranch.

Men on foot—who will tell you what a skilled job they do—are also there to drive the cattle, and they walk along with the *cabestros*. Experience dictates that they should proceed calmly, no faster than a normal walking pace, so that the *cabestros* trot along quietly without getting alarmed or upset, panicking the bulls and starting a stampede, thus creating complete chaos.

Some stockmen are highly expert, not to say geniuses, at driving bulls with *cabestros*. On a visit to a ranch in Albacete, I was astonished, dumbstruck with admiration even, to see one of the stockbreeder's sons herding cattle exactly as if he were doing it with *cabestros*. In actual fact that day I assumed that he was also playing the role of the bullocks, since as far as I could see the ranch did not possess a single *cabestro*.

The task in hand was corraling a fair number of cows and calves, plus four bulls, and he did this in a very short space of time and with irreproachable efficiency. He used everything he had at his disposal, and that came down to his voice, his arms, and his legs, doing it in such a way that to shouts of "je" and "juy," "amoninó" and "jiamó-jiamó" the animals awaited their orders and seemed to understand everything that he said. Then, still shouting orders and instructions— "jatuoró," "julijoló," "jujijijó"—he started waving his arms about and began to run. He ran more than the cows, the calves, and the four bulls, on feet that were fleeter than those of *cabestros*.

When he had finished, flushed and dripping with sweat, I was on the point of giving him an effusive embrace, so impressed was I. But I refrained and simply said:

"You must be dead beat."

He replied:

"No, I'm not. Why?"

"I don't know, kid… Just watching you has given me a thirst."

"That's easily fixed."

As he spoke he ran off into the house, and came straight back with a couple of bottles of beer. He drank his in one gulp.

This young man was a prodigy of nature. He would have been a star on the Olympic field.

Herding is not only a question of driving cattle but also of avoiding accidents with them.

Fights between bulls can be one problem; another is that they can hurt themselves or break their horns if they knock against anything hard. Some bulls use trees as scratching posts, and certain stockbreeders maintain that rubbing wears down their horns and leaves them with odd-looking patches, as if someone had shaved them. This belief of stockbreeders is not well founded, however. Horns are diamond-hard and if a bull were to damage them by rubbing he would have to be rubbing solidly for a year or more.

In the Trigueros district, we were touring Celestino Cuadri's ranch, which is one of the best ranches today. Cuadri's bulls are among the few that have their own distinct personality. Anyone who has set eyes on a Cuadri bull will always be able to recognize another quite easily. It is a little like the royal house of Bourbon, who retained the same facial features down the generations. Many of the cattle on the El Pardo ranch also display this tendency.

It is not that Cuadri's black bulls are particularly distinguished. Better bulls than his are to be seen on almost any ranch. Nevertheless, these bulls have their own distinct personality: serious, profound, and hunched up in their shoulders. They also possess indisputable fighting class, proof of the enthusiasm and genuineness that the stockbreeder brings to the *tienta*, selecting both stud bulls and cows, and their offspring.

It is thought that a bull's strength and its coat are enough to indicate its class, and the stockbreeder would do well to work on these basic criteria. Bulls that in their physique and in their coat show traces of the original strain do so because they carry these features in their blood, and they or their predecessors should be used as breeding stock. The old Concha and Sierra strains, which are today in different hands, still display unusual, light-colored coats, as does the Cobaleda strain, which is referred to as "white foot." These are only two examples.

The "white foot" cattle were purchased by Victorino Martín, who is perhaps the best stockbreeder of the second half of the 20th century. He has now established a new ranch. Victorino Martín's own bulls, which are known simply as "los victorinos," also possess a distinct personality and can be very easily identified as coming from his ranch.

This is also the case with stock from the legendary Miura ranch—the most famous in the entire history of bullfighting—and some of its animals bear the stamp of the establishment. Not always, though. In certain fights, Miura bulls have not been true to form. Once in the bullring, they seem to lack personality, which makes one wonder if the stockbreeder uses more than one criterion for selection.

Bulls belonging to the strain bred at Santa Coloma, one of the most highly prized strains among all those that exist, are similarly distinctive, and stud bulls from the herd have been used to establish and improve stock on many ranches. The stock of the heirs of Hernández Plá is one of the most truly elite as far as class and power are concerned, and I am not afraid to declare them among my favorites. Back in the 1980s, there was a bull named Capitán—black-coated and medium-sized, naturally—whose inexhaustible power made him a sensation. This Capitán, and the young bull Horquillero, from the ranch run by Isaías and Tulio Vázquez, who appeared in the bullring in Madrid in the 1950s, are probably the bravest bulls that I have ever seen in all my long and active time as an aficionado.

My visit to Cuadri's ranch, in the Huelvan countryside around Trigueros, was in a professional capacity. I had come with the aim of writing an article—which appeared in *El País* a few days later—and the stockbreeder was kind and patient enough to tell us about every single set of bulls that were ready to fight that year. With his head stockman, Fernando Cuadri rode into the enclosures on horseback, and the photographer and I, in a pickup truck driven by the stockman's brother, kept to the outside.

Each set of bulls was in a different enclosure and those who were on horseback trotted off in search of the bulls, which would sometimes be found beneath distant clumps of trees, where they sometimes ended up when they wandered off. Keeping their voices low and making the minimum movement, they managed to do what they wanted; the bulls obediently came toward us, stopped in front of us, and went back to grazing, browsing, or sniffing the air aloofly. When we had finished looking at them, the horsemen gave a couple of shouts and waved their arms about, and the bulls wandered off as quietly as they had come.

When we reached the fourth or fifth enclosure—where the fourth or fifth set of bulls was kept—something very significant happened. Fernando Cuadri and his head stockman were riding toward the far end of the estate where the bulls had gone; after a short while they returned with the bulls, bringing them to us by the same simple methods and as quietly and calmly as before.

A barrier separated the enclosure from the road, and the photographer, the stockbreeder's brother, and I were naturally keeping to the far side, which was the safe side. The barrier was no makeshift affair—it was solidly built of stone and cement.

The stockbreeder and the head stockman drew near, as did the bulls, which began to mill around near the barrier. But this was not the whole herd, since a straggler had fallen behind some way back; although they called to him, waved their arms at him, and rounded him up with their horses, he was reluctant to come near and they left him to his own devices. When we had finished looking at the bulls, we told the stockbreeder and he gave the bulls their marching orders, which they obeyed. But they had hardly gone any distance when the straggler became enraged, thundered over to where we were standing behind the wall and took a flying jump, with the obvious idea of reaching the road. He gave us a terrific fright and we dived for cover behind the truck. There we stayed, all three of us cowering at the sound of the bull furiously butting the wall. I asked the stockbreeder:

"Should we get into the truck?"

"No, be quiet," he replied. "Keep absolutely quiet and hopefully he won't see us."

Hidden and trembling we waited for the danger to pass, for a few minutes that seemed an eternity since we could hear the stockbreeder and his head stockman moving about and shouting in an attempt to drive the furious creature away. This they managed to do after a while and we were told we could come out. We went back to the scene and froze in our tracks: the bull had managed to knock down part of the wall with his horns and the hole was so large that he could easily have jumped through.

"Did he break his horns?" we asked the stockbreeder.

"No," he replied. "They're quite unharmed." We looked carefully at that bull's horns. Of course, he could easily have broken them off when he attacked the wall, but he was lucky to have sustained no injury; we could see no sign of any damage whatsoever to his horns, which looked diamond-hard.

When certain stockbreeders try to explain why bulls reach the bullring with a "shaven" appearance—with their horns unusually short or blunt—they suggest that this must be because the bulls rub against trees, rocks, or the ground. These explanations seem to be very strange. After the incident on Cuadri's ranch, they seem even more unlikely.

Those bulls that were being kept in the enclosures were ready for the bullring that year, segregated in groups of six, for the various bullrings that the stockbreeder was contracted to supply. The bullfight that took place in Madrid a month later was an exceptional event.

It was still wintertime, although spring was already coming to the Huelvan countryside; the meadows were covered in fresh grass and the sun shone brightly.

The way that bulls are kept in the months before they are due to fight is important. To ensure that they reach peak condition, their diet is varied and monitored, and care is taken that they remain calm and content. In this author's modest opinion, the exercise that some stockbreeders swear by, holding that this is good for the bulls, is counterproductive. Other stockbreeders agree.

It is certain that long walks are conducive to the peak form that is needed in the ring, when the time comes. It was once the practice to position feeding-troughs so that the bulls had to walk long distances to reach them and also their drink afterward. To make them gallop about, on the other hand—which cannot be done without alarming and frightening them—is another matter altogether.

The mindset of the fighting bull is ultimately almost no different from any other untamed animal. I once took the opportunity to observe the behavior of the wild animals of the African savanna. None of them showed much evidence of exercising. The lions, for example, spent the day lying in the sun or gamboling about in the shade. Sometimes one would get up, stretch its whole body while digging its claws into the ground, have a quick wash and flop down someplace else, which it found more comfortable or warmer. At other times, the wanderer would return to the family group to play with his mate or with the cubs.

Of course, if anything caught their attention, they would become alert, sniffing the air with every muscle tensed. Wild animals all have a fine sense of smell, keen eyesight, and indomitable ferocity. When a lion has its prey in its sights, it strikes like a bolt of lightning. And it does not need to do fitness exercises of any kind to give it sufficient range and stamina for the kill.

Class and good health are all that a bull needs to perform in the ring with the physique and stamina that are necessary for the fight.

Shortly before the day of the bullfight, bulls are driven out of the enclosure and into the loading area. This is where the *cabestros* (bullocks) come in useful. In the old days, bulls were driven to the bullring across country, with an escort of stockmen, and this was a kind of military operation that could sometimes last for weeks. Today, bulls are transported to the bullring loaded on to trucks in individual crates. According to bullfighting historians, the first bull to travel in a crate, at the end of the 19th century, was in Barcelona.

The loading area on a ranch consists of an arrangement of small enclosures, passageways, and a ramp leading to the crate. The bull enters the crate, which is closed by a drop-down gate. On arrival at the bullring, it is unloaded by a similar process and released into a corral, where it will stay, with *cabestros* for company, until the time comes for a veterinary examination. It is then taken and shut in the bullpen. Traditionally, the bull is shut in the bullpen at noon on the day of the fight and kept there until the bugle sounds to announce the opening of the bullpen door and its exit into the ring. In the darkness, a rosette in the colors indicating its breeder will be pinned to the bull's shoulder. The sting of the barbed dart, the blinding light that hits it in the eyes when the door is opened, and the roar of the crowd that greets its appearance will stimulate its aggression. The bull will shoot into the ring at a gallop, enraged and looking for a fight.

And so the bulls arrive in their crates, to be unloaded at the bullring.

There are hundreds of bullrings in Spain, most of them extremely inconvenient and uncomfortable; and many of them, partly if not wholly through their own fault,

are extremely dilapidated. This is because they are so antiquated, and badly maintained by their proprietors; all too often no money has been invested in badly needed upkeep or rebuilding.

Many bullrings are public property or are run by institutions, such as committees, town halls, or charitable foundations. The bullring as a political investment is also important and should be emphasized. Politicians were mindful of popular interest in bullfighting, and to satisfy this they had to build bullrings. As elsewhere, they were responsible for welfare payments for which they had to find a source, and funds turned out to be scarce; some of the income from gate money was reinvested, partly to meet the cost of construction of the bullring and partly for its maintenance, the rest being used to fund those welfare payments.

Many charitable institutions were funded by bullfighting. Among them are the Casas de Misericordia; the one in Pamplona is extremely well run, and to this day provides shelter and medical care for elderly people in the city using income from the annual bull-running festival. Many hospitals also owe their existence to gate money taken at bullrings. Another good example is the provincial bullring in Madrid, which launched the traditional Corrida de Beneficienca (benefit bullfight), the most famous in the world. Displays of horsemanship were funded by income from the bullrings owned by these foundations; those that take place in Seville and Ronda have developed a particular character on account of their history and the way they are performed.

In the early days of bullfighting, bullrings were temporary structures that could be put up and taken down again. They were made of wood, and the oldest are reputed to be the Real Maestranza and the Resolana bullrings. The former is in Seville, and dates from the end of the 17th century. It stood near the Guadalquivir river on the spot known as the Arenal. Others were built a few years later and in 1761 work began on what is known simply as the Maestranza; this was a rentable temple to bullfighting. The Madrid bullring was built of wood in an out-of-the-way location outside the city walls, near the Puerta de Alcalá. Another was built in stone in the same place, and as time went on there was a succession of bullrings, the most important of which is the one known today as Plaza Vieja. It was superseded in 1935 by the Monumental, built in the Las Ventas del Espíritu Santo district, and this is the one that is still in use today. Many aficionados refer to the Monumental bullring in Las Ventas as "the first in the world" and think of it as the ultimate center of bullfighting. The Real Maestranza in Ronda—which is perhaps the most attractive of all bullrings—was built in 1758. Others followed, among them those in Zaragoza and Aranjuez, also in the 18th century, and those in Valencia, Cadiz, and Puerto de Santa María, in the 19th century.

An index of 40 bullrings appears below. The selection is made on account of their historical or contemporary importance, or of their being distinctive in some way.

ALBACETE

A bullring was built here in 1828. It remained in use until 1917, when the present bullring, with seating for 12,000 spectators, was erected. A major *feria* (a series of bullfights that takes place during the town's festival) is held in September each year. Other bullfights also take place here.

ALICANTE

The bullring was built in 1847. Spacious and well laid out, it has seating for as many as 15,000 spectators. A major *feria* takes place in June. Other bullfights are also held here.

ALMERÍA

The bullring was built in 1888, with seating for about 10,000 spectators. A major *feria* takes place at the end of August.

ARANJUEZ

Built by royal decree in 1796, this bullring is extremely attractive, with a rich, historic atmosphere, although remarkably uncomfortable. Works to improve and strengthen the building were carried out in honor of its bicentenary.

BADAJOZ

The bullring was built around the year 1900 with seating for about 8,000 spectators. Bullfights take place there at various times of the year, in addition to the *feria*.

BARCELONA

Barcelona is a major center of bullfighting in Spain. Its Monumental bullring is one of three such in the world (the others are in Madrid and in Mexico). The bullring in the district of Barceloneta was superseded by that at Las Arenas, built in 1900 on the Plaza de España. It is now closed, although it is in working order. The Monumental was opened in 1914 and has undergone various improvements since. It has seating for about 20,000 spectators.

BILBAO

The present bullring is probably the most comfortable in Spain. It has stands with wide seats giving a perfect view in all directions. In the 1970s it superseded the city's old bullring, which dated back to the 19th century and had suffered serious fire damage. A major *feria*, known as the Corridas Generales, takes place here in August.

BURGOS

This city has a long bullfighting tradition and there has been a bullring here since 1860. An interesting *feria* takes place in June.

CÁCERES

The bullring dates from 1846. The city's large population of bullfighting fans supports festivals throughout the year, as well as the traditional *feria*. Like other bullrings in the Extremadura region, this one attracts many Portuguese aficionados.

COLMENAR VIEJO

This town, in Madrid province, has some of the keenest bullfighting fans in the country, no doubt as a result of the region's deep-rooted cattle farming tradition. The *feria*, which takes place between late August and early September in a brand new bullring, features some top-class bullfighting, in that the crowd demands bulls of serious strength and power.

CUENCA

There has been a bullring here since the mid-19th century. The present bullring dates from 1926. The city holds a traditional *feria*.

GRANADA

The bullfighting tradition here goes back a long way. The bullring that was built in the early 19th century was seriously damaged first by fire and later by a storm that destroyed its upper part. The new bullring opened in 1928.

GUADALAJARA

The first bullring here was built in 1850. The bullring now hosts a short *feria* in September, which attracts big names.

HUELVA

An interesting *feria* takes place here in August, although it is not as important as might be expected given that Huelva is located in the heart of bull-raising country, amid major ranches.

HUESCA

This historic bullring hosts only a small number of bullfights, almost all of them constituting a short *feria*.

JAÉN

One of the reasons why the city's *feria* is important is that, taking place in mid-October, it is the last of the season. There has been a bullring here since 1847.

JEREZ DE LA FRONTERA

Founded in 1839, this is one of the most important bullrings in southern Spain, famous for the bullfights held here as competitions between ranches. The Feria del Caballo (horse fair) has also become a key event.

LOGROÑO

The old bullring, which dates from 1862, was superseded by another, built in 1915. The *feria* here, which takes place in September, is one of the most important of the season.

MADRID

The city's oldest bullring was built by Philip IV, near the royal palace of Buen Retiro. Over time, several others were built, most notably the one known today as the Vieja Plaza de Toros de Madrid, which stood on the Carretera de Aragón. Major bullfighting festivals were held there. It was the scene of the golden age of bullfighting, and the festival of bullfights that took place there was the high point of the city's fiesta. It was replaced by the Monumental, in Las Ventas, which hosted a series of benefit bullfights in 1931 and did not come into regular use until 1935. Built to a design by José Gómez Ortega, known as Gallito or alternatively as Joselito (or Joselito el Gallo) it has a splendid array of buildings and other rooms, with the needs of the fight a priority, and the aficionados of the time thought it very spacious and comfortable. People in those days must have been thinner and shorter (since the 1930s, it is true that people have become larger) because today's spectators complain that the seats are too narrow for comfort. The Feria de San Isidro, which runs for almost a month, takes place here in May; the Feria de Otoño is held between the end of the September and the beginning of October; and the brief Feria de la Communidad Madrileña happens between the end of April and the beginning of May; there are also bullfights every Sunday and on public holidays from May to the end of October. Over the season this bullring hosts about 80 bullfights and *novilladas* (bullfights using young bulls).

MÁLAGA

This city has a long-standing bullfighting tradition. The first bullring here was built in the 18th century. A major *feria*, considered to be a classic in the bullfighting calendar, takes place in August.

MURCIA

There has been a bullring here since 1886. An interesting *feria* takes place in September.

PALENCIA

This bullring attracts some of the keenest crowds in the country. There has been a bullring here since the early 19th century. The *feria* draws a large number of aficionados from across the region.

PALMA DE MALLORCA

The original bullring was built here in 1856. Few bullfights have taken place here in some years, although a recent recovery has started.

Pamplona

Although bullfighting has a keen following here and this is bullfighting country, a location that is sometimes held to be epitome of bullfighting culture, Pamplona did not have a stone-built bullring until well into the 19th century. The present bullring is large and comfortable, with seating for almost 18,000 spectators, and it is filled to capacity during the *feria*. The Feria de San Fermín, with bull-running in the mornings, is one of the most important and best known bullfighting events in the world.

Puerto de Santa María

"Toros en el Puerto" is a famous strap line on the advertising billboards of this town in Cadiz province. The highly historic bullfighting annals of Puerto de Santa María go back to the 18th century. The present-day bullring, built in 1880, is large, having one of the widest arenas and seating for about 15,000 spectators. The most important bullfights to take place here are held in July and August.

Ronda

The Real Maestranza de Caballería, built in 1785, is a beautiful and architecturally important building. The traditional Corrida Goyesca is held here every September and those who take part, dressed in Goyaesque costume, are among the most celebrated figures in the bull-fighting world.

Salamanca

The city's *feria*, which takes place in September, is another important event in the Spanish bullfighting season. Bullfights were held in the Plaza Mayor before the city's first bullring was built in 1865. In 1892, having become dilapidated and too small to cope with the increased population, it was superseded by a larger, better-designed bullring.

Santander

The city has a very long bullfighting tradition, and there has been a bullring here since the mid-19th century. Yet for many years the small number of fans made it unviable to mount a permanent program of bullfights, and this kept the city out of the national limelight. Thanks to financial aid over the last ten years, spectator numbers have increased, and a very promising *feria* takes place in August.

Segovia

The city has a large, well-appointed bullring, which hosts a short *feria* and other bullfights throughout the season.

Seville

The Maestranza is one of the most handsomely proportioned, pleasing, and attractive bullrings in the world. Various bullfights take place here throughout the season, including *novilladas* (bullfights using young bulls), but the high point of the year is the Feria de Abril, which takes place over two or more weeks in the month of April, and which features some top-class bulls and bullfighters. Seville's *feria* and Madrid's Feria de San Isidro mark the high point of the bullfighting year. In September the Maestranza also hosts the Feria de San Miguel, which has now been reduced to two or three series of bullfights. The bullring at El Arenal, together with the Maestranza, which preceded it, were among the first to be built in Spain. By the 1920s, Seville also had a Monumental bullring, which, like Madrid's, was built to a design by Joselito and as the result of his initiative. However, it was in use for only a very short time, being unable to compete with the Maestranza, which was always preferred by aficionados.

Talavera de la Reina

A short *feria*, which attracts some of the most prominent names, takes place here in September, with another event in May. The bullring owes its renown, however, to its unhappy associations: on May 16, 1920, it was here that Joselito, perhaps the most versatile of all bull-fighters, was fatally gored.

TARRAGONA

The city has an excellent bullring of ample dimensions, in which bullfights take place throughout the summer.

TERUEL

This bullring was built in 1850, and subsequently restored and modernized. A *feria* takes place in August.

TOLEDO

This is one of the country's classic bullrings, as much on account of its history as because of its location; being close to Madrid, aficionados from the capital come to watch bullfights here. The principal *feria* is held at Corpus Christi, which in Toledo is a major secular and religious festival. Toledo's bullring opened on August 18, 1866, and because of its age it is not among the most comfortable.

VALENCIA

Valencia is one of Spain's major bullfighting cities. Two important *ferias* are held here: the Feria de la Fallas, in March, and the Feria de San Jaime, in July. During the 1980s, the city also hosted the Feria de la Communidad Valenciana, in October. The Feria de San Jaime, along with Madrid's great *ferias*, became the most important event in the bullfighting world, and the most important bullfighters would take part in it. Bullfighting festivals were already taking place in Valencia in the 17th century; the bullrings at that time were temporary wooden structures but by the 18th century they were of masonry construction. In 1860, a stone-built bullring was raised. It is an extremely handsome building, based on the design of the circus of Flavius Marcellus and equipped with generously proportioned outbuildings. For many years its corrals were more spacious and more conveniently positioned than those of any other bullring in Spain. It has seating for 16,000 spectators and is located in the city center, off the Calle Xátiva, a few yards from the Plaza del Ayuntamiento and stone's throw from the railroad station.

VALLADOLID

The city's first bullring opened in 1834. This was superseded by a larger, more modern bullring in 1890. In September, the present bullring in Valladolid hosts one of the most important *ferias* in the country.

VIRTUDES

Virtudes is endowed with one of the strangest imaginable bullrings. It is rectangular, with three sides being taken up by seating and the fourth being closed off by the wall of a convent building. Few bullfights, none of them significant, take place here.

VITORIA

The Feria de la Virgen de la Blanca, in early August, is a long-standing event in the bullfighting season. The original bullring, which was constructed in 1851, was superseded by another, built in 1888.

ZAMORA

Zamora's first bullring was built in 1879, and was subsequently rebuilt several times. A *feria* takes place here.

ZARAGOZA

There was a bullring here as early as 1764. The present one, designed by Pignatelli, is one of the most modern in Spain. It is also the first to be enclosed; the removable roof comes in useful in October, when wind and rain are likely, and also when the *feria* takes place. Bullfights are held throughout the season, and come the Feria del Pilar, Zaragoza's bullring is the focus of world attention. On account of the quality and number of bullfights that it comprises, this *feria* is one of the most significant in the bullfighting year.

The bullring must have certain features. The arena must be circular, for good reason. A circular fence that completely encloses the arena will give the bull no opportunity for retreat into a corner, and prevents it from returning to the same spot.

The bullring—for which there are a number of words in Spanish, including *ruedo, redondel, círculo,* and *coso taurino*—is directly linked to various other buildings, which are also arranged in a particular way. Joselito el Gallo, who had an exact and thorough understanding of bullfighting, developed the ideal layout for these peripheral buildings, which are to be found at many bullrings.

The Monumental bullring in Madrid, also known as Las Ventas, is one such. It is a model of a bullring meticulously laid out to meet the needs of bullfighting. There are three entrances into the ring: one for the *cuadrillas* (matador's assistants), one giving access to the slaughterhouse, and one to the bullpen. The fourth entrance, known as the *puerta grande* or *puerta de Madrid,* is the principal one. It opens only twice, at most, during the course of a bullfight: once to allow the *alguacilillos* (officials who lead the parade and present the trophies to the bullfighters), and again when, if he is acclaimed, the victorious matador makes a triumphant return to the ring on the shoulders of his supporters.

For some years now, this door has been used by the picadors when they enter the ring for the first phase of the bullright. This is not only wrong but truly barbaric. It seems that the promoters allow it because they think it takes too long for the picadors to come through the *puerta de cuadrillas* and arrive in the ring to start the first phase, and that this allows the crowd to entertain themselves by protesting about the bull's power. Quite apart from the fact that this justification is unacceptable, whoever allowed this innovation was revealing that he had no idea about bullfighting. It is a serious matter that the very people who play such a central role in bullfighting should have such a poor understanding of it.

At Las Ventas, the *puerta de cuadrillas* opens on the side of the bullring that receives the sun, in the section known as number 4. This is well away from the barrier behind which the bullfighter takes refuge, located between sections 8 and 9, where the first phase of the bullfight usually takes place. This is for strictly technical reasons: the bull's fighting spirit is best displayed when the first phase is executed as far away from the entrance to the bullpen as possible, countering any tendency the bull may have to return to it.

In a well-conducted bullfight, no sooner has the bull been released into the ring than the bullfighter capes the bull to focus it. The presiding officer waves a white flag, which is the order for the bugle to sound, giving the signal for the picadors to come into the ring.

The bullfighter stands in front of the focused bull and makes a series of passes, usually *verónicas* (executed with a large cape); moving toward the center of the ring, he shows off as much as he can, giving time for the picador to arrive and at the same time vacating the space where the picador needs to be. If the matador has done all this to plan, when the passes have been performed—usually with the *media verónica*—he leaves the bull and then moves quickly to the left of the horse; the picador incites the bull; the bull then charges and the first strike of the lance is delivered.

When the picadors enter the ring by the *puerta grande*, the whole process is spoiled. The fact that the *puerta grande* is only a few yards from the spot where the *suerte de varas* takes place makes for great disarray. After the matador has made passes at the bull with the cape, the assistants have to step in to drive the bull away, so that the *puerta grande* can be opened without any risk that the bull will rush toward it. The picador then enters the ring on his great Percheron and, while he is positioning himself, the assistants concentrate on diverting the bull's attention, close to the barrier at section 1. When the picador is in position, they bring the bull back for the second phase of the bullfight. The result of this confused procedure is a lot of unnecessary dashing about, which wastes time, is quite without merit, and spoils the beauty of bullfighting.

Throughout the entire history of bullfighting and up to a couple of decades ago, the person who received the bull when it was released in the ring was an assistant, who brought it to a halt by briefly showing it the cape. This phase, which demanded courage and dexterity, is of enormous value; it was executed with great panache and fired the crowd's enthusiasm. Bullfighting is something that comprises skill and excitement in equal measure.

Veteran aficionados remember assistants who received the bull single-handed. Many of them had to acknowledge the crowd's applause cap in hand. Gorings did occur, however. Running a bull single-handed was precisely how Coli met his end, in Madrid, back in the 1950s. The bullfighter fell to the ground, and the bull ran the unfortunate Coli right through the kidneys. The wounded man received swift medical attention but was dead on arrival at hospital.

Aficionados say that some assistants who fought bulls single-handed seem to be born naturals. That is why those who have seen this phase performed would like to see it revived. Today it is almost always the matador who receives the bull first, and if any assistants enter the ring they will not take the bull on single-handed.

Another way of receiving the bull is with bold displays of bravery. These usually involve techniques known as *larga afarolada* or *larga cambiada*. The bull can also be received by the bullfighter on his knees. Some do this "*a porta gayola*"—that is, right in front of the door leading to the bullpens.

The technique of receiving a bull "*a porta gayola*" requires that the bullfighter position himself between the first line of picadors and the door leading to the bullpens; technically he should be in the center of the ring. When the door to the bullpen is opened, the furious bull surges out of the darkness, and the first thing he meets is a man down on his knees. You would expect the bull to run straight over him, but the kneeling man is a skilled bullfighter who can keep his nerve; he deflects the thunderous assault by waving the cape, which takes the full brunt of the powerful charge.

The *larga cambiada* can be executed either standing or kneeling. It involves the bullfighter inciting the bull with the cape held to one side and forcing it to switch to the other side by whipping the cape around. The *larga afarolada* is a similar technique except that the bullfighter passes the cape over his head. Moves in which the cape is passed over the head are known as *farol*. If the move is executed with the *muleta* (the red cape attached to a stick), it is known as *afarolado*.

Bullfighting terminology is quite easily explained. The cape known as the *verónica* is named for the devout woman who held out her veil to Jesus Christ so that he might wipe his face on his way to the Crucifixion.

To execute a *verónica*, the bullfighter stands in front of the bull, slightly to one side of it, with the leg nearest the animal to the fore. When he shows it the cape (in a gesture similar to that used by the Biblical woman), the bull charges and just as it is about to reach the cape the bullfighter steps forward, simultaneously bringing the rear leg forward, and lets the bull surge through.

The bullfighter is then in the same position as he was to start with, except that the bull is now facing in the opposite direction. That is to say, the bullfighter's leg that is the nearest to the bull is to the fore; once again he holds up the cape and repeats the move with the same technique. Using this classic technique, the bullfighter can execute a continuous succession of moves, gaining ground on the bull with each one so that the bull will feel dominated.

The best way to conclude a series of such moves is with the *media verónica*. This is executed in the same way as the *verónica* except that, as the bull reaches the cape, the bullfighter whips it up into the air with a flourish and holds it across his hips with both hands; the bull meanwhile describes a very tight semicircle, a maneuver that is extremely tiring.

Gitanillo de Triana, known as Curro Puya—who died in the 1940s after being gored—is revered as the bullfighter who was the most skillful with the *verónica*. Other aficionados could name present-day bullfighters who have given sublime displays with the *verónica*, including such figures as Chicuelo, Cagancho, Pepe Luis Vázquez, Antonio Bienvenida, Antonio Ordóñez, Rafael Ortega, Curro Romero, and Rafael de Paula. The list does not stop there; there have been other consummate manipulators of the *verónica*, who will all be remembered for their sublime contribution.

There are no rules governing the precise way in which bullfighters use the *verónica* or any other technique when the bull first enters the ring, although of all the moves that have been established in the long history of bullfighting it is the most clearly defined. The same could be said about the repertoire of *quites* (moves to draw the bull away)—of these, more later.

We now move on to the phase in which the bull is jabbed. This phase is a key part of the bullfight, and for considerable periods of time in the history of bullfighting it was overwhelmingly prominent, to an extent that on posters advertising bullfights the names of the picadors were printed in larger type than those of the matadors. As the bullfighting fiesta evolved, the matadors became the most prominent players, and the picadors' renown was relegated to second place, even though the *suerte de varas* (the phase in the bullfight when the picador weakens the bull with his lance) never lost its fundamental importance.

In the old days there was no demarcation line in the ring marking off the picadors' area from that of the bull. It was the picadors' misdemeanor that made it necessary for lines to the drawn; so that the bull should not bring them down, they would execute the phase without moving away from the fence. The crowd and the bullfighters themselves demanded, many times unsuccessfully, that they go further out into the ring. Negotiations took place between both sides and the result was that the picadors would go further out to jab the bull, but only for a set distance away from the barrier, which would be fixed by tracing a circle on the ground. Today's crowds hurl abuse at picadors who break out of the circle, holding it to be an unfair advantage assumed by those who were demanding not to have to go beyond a certain point to preserve their own safety.

Another problem that has yet to be resolved concerns the position of the bulls during the *suerte de varas*. Many bullfighters would like to see them almost underneath the horses, but this give the bull no advantage at all nor any chance to show its fighting spirit. It was Domingo Ortega who suggested that another circle be drawn, running parallel inside the existing circle; the space between the lines would be a no-man's land, with the picadors on the side nearest the barrier and the bull on the other.

The time it takes for a bull to charge, its speed, and its determination make for an exciting spectacle and are a measure of its fighting spirit. Some bulls take a while to charge, some with an apparent lack of aggression, some seem to hesitate; all these reactions, among others, are signs of possible docility. Some bulls react to the smallest thing and the crowd roars if they turn tail and charge across to the other side of the bullring, possibly trying to find their way back to the bullpen.

A bull endowed with strength and fighting spirit will give an impressive performance that will have the crowd rise to its feet. A bull endowed with strength and fighting spirit is quick to charge, sticking its head beneath the horse and lifting it with its horns. It will not toss its head when it is jabbed with the lance, which a skillful picador will have plunged into its shoulders, however, it will seek revenge against its enemy; it will lower its hindquarters, puff out its great neck, and will charge again and again, powerfully, aggressively, and fixedly. This goes on until the picador turns his horse to the right, and the bullfighter shows the bull the cape to the left, reclaiming the bull's attention, and executing the *quite*, receiving the charge in its folds.

The move is then repeated. It is well known that many bulls show great fighting spirit when they are jabbed for the first time but may not react in the same way the second or third time, and turn out to be meek. To gauge a bull's true

fighting spirit, experience has shown that it should be jabbed at least three times, and this is why previous rules stipulated this minimum. Unfortunately, modern regulations limit it to two.

Any bull that takes at least three jabs with unflinching bravery has already begun to deserve to be spared to fight another day. These three jabs with the lance must of course be given with some degree of care. No bull can sustain an indefinite number—how many will be determined by the physical strength of the bull.

The *suerte de varas* was not designed to break the animal's spirit but to wound it so as to provoke its fury. Regulations dictated that the bull should be jabbed in the shoulders, a conspicuously bulging part of the body that contains no vital organs and which bleeds profusely when the hide is pierced.

Everything about the *suerte de varas* was very carefully thought out and the authority that presided over bullfights was vigilant that nothing be done to excess. But that was in the old days. The *suerte de varas* has degenerated and today hardly anyone jabs from the right, nor aims the lance at the shoulders, nor turns the horse away to bring the phase to a close; instead, when the bull charges, the picador jabs the lance into the spine, turns his horse so that it circles the bull, and traps it against the barrier, turning the whole procedure into nothing less than butchery. Far from inciting the bull's fury, all that this method of jabbing accomplishes is to destroy some of the bull's vital organs; this gives the bull no chance at all, nor can it show any fighting spirit—a single jab sounds the bull's death knell.

This method of jabbing the bull also impedes the proper execution of the *quites*. After each of the three minimum jabs of the picador's lance, it used to be customary for great bullfighters to execute a *quite*, and they would do this in elaborate fashion, each rivaling the other. Thus three regulation jabs of the lance were followed by three inspired *quites*; by the end of this phase, the crowd had already witnessed a great spectacle.

Bullfighters have a wide range of lances at their disposal, from which they can select according to their use and according to the bull's form. As it has evolved, bullfighting has constantly produced new moves, which may be imaginative variations on existing moves or newly created ones. Bullfighting with the *verónica* is very well suited to *quites* but so are the *largas* in their three different versions— the *larga cambiada*, the *larga afarolada*, and the *larga cordobesa*—and also the *tijerilla*, formerly known as "*a lo chatre*," the *tapatía*, the *talaverana*, the *rogerina*, the *fregolina*, the *saltillera*, the *gaonera*, the *vitolina*, the *chicuelina*, and many more (named for their creators or the town where they were born) plus the final moves in each phase, which are also very varied (prominent among them are the staunch *media verónica*, the light *revolera*, and the baroque *serpentina*).

I am convinced that the *suerte de banderillas* (the second phase of the bullfight, in which the *banderillas* is stuck into the bull's neck) is one of the most brilliant inventions in bullfighting. Present-day bullfighters are sometimes told, however, that *banderillas* (barbed darts) "don't serve any purpose at all."

Whoever introduced the *suerte de banderillas* into the bullfight did so for sound reasons. It is only to be expected that a bull will lose its aggressive edge after being subjected to jabs with the lance. This is not so much through physical exhaustion as through the tendency to charge at relatively short distances. Basically an animal that acts through intuition, the bull adjusts to fighting within a radius of a few yards, a space within which it need not move any distance, but has to launch repeated attacks against the person who is meting out the punishment.

It is widely known that a bull will only react to punishment; this is the principle on which *tientas* are conducted, and it continues to apply in the bullring. It is, therefore, a matter of inflicting light punishment that will provoke it to revert to charging from a distance. This is achieved with a barbed dart. A man will incite it from a distance and when the bull charges the barbed dart is sunk into its shoulders. Intuitively the bull understands that the man calling to it in the distance is the cause of the pain and every time it sees him he will charge at him again. Doing this three times is enough to wind the bull up again.

This is the reason why the *suerte de banderillas* became part of the bullfight, and its value was clear in that it produced finely executed and exciting jabs. The earliest *banderilleros* only stuck in a single barbed dart. At first this was a rudimentary act; it later came to consist of sinking the barbed dart into the bull's back and pulling it out again. Later still a specific technique was used, which upped the danger, the excitement, and the skill required to pull it off.

The job of the *banderillero* is nothing less than a profession but there are matadors who also carry out the duties of the *banderillero* with great displays of skill. Some of them are masters of the art. Pepe Bienvenida and Pepe Dominguín stand head and shoulders above those matadors of the post-Civil War period who have been brilliant exponents of this move. Just as in moves with the hand-held cape and the cape attached to a pole, an impressive repertoire is attached to the art of *banderillear*, which is deployed according to the bull's form and the skill of the *banderilleros*.

Historians tell how the romantic bullfighter El Gordito, the inventor of the *quiebro* (literally "the dodge"), worked into his *suertes de banderillas* some incredible displays. For example, he would call to the bull, inciting it to go for him and as it ran he would suddenly hold out his hand in a signal to stop, and so the bull would stop. Or the bull would be standing still, and he would tiptoe around it repeatedly without the bull charging until at a given moment he would make a sign meaning "follow me," and the bull would follow him as if it were tame. Some other master *banderilleros* also performed these feats. Luis Francisco Esplá has done so many times, holding the crowd in thrall, although it remains to be seen whether future historians will continue to rate him highly.

The best *banderilleros* have a highly accurate perception of the bull's form. Any bullfighter who cannot make out a bull's form will never be a good *banderillero*. There are today some *banderilleros* who make up for their shortcomings with twists and turns, frenetic dashing about and pompous acknowledgments to the crowd.

The skilled *banderillero* knows the point at which the bull will retire and when it will come forward, as well as precisely how it will pitch forward; he knows whether it will charge soon or late, and whether it will do so at speed or more slowly. If he executes the move correctly in relation to the animal's form, and if he leans right over to stick the *banderilleros* at the very crest of the bull's back, he will have taken the art of *banderillar* to the height of perfection.

The bell sounds and the final phase of the bullfight is about to begin.

The matador dedicates the bull and stands ready to make a series of passes with the red cape.

Excitement is at a peak. The moment has come when bull and matador confront each other in the empty expanse of the bullring.

The bull, now bristling with *banderillas*, enters a new phase. Having been lanced, it is not charging with the ardor it displayed when it first entered the ring; now everything moves at a slower pace. This allows the matador to perform his moves with measured poise. Not that everything necessarily goes smoothly; after the vicissitudes of the fight, the bull sometimes becomes irritable and dangerous, charging unexpectedly.

The bull may come to a standstill in the middle of a move, it may give in at the least expected moment, it may charge with its head held high, or it may appear defeated yet turn nasty again in the middle of a move.

A bull is always dangerous. Even the noblest of bulls can cause disaster if the matador makes an error of judgment. A mistake sometimes results from hesitation, from choosing the wrong position in the ring, or from a small display of ill temper when beginning the charge.

Disaster—anything from a tossing or a somersault to a goring—happens in a split second and is over in a flash.

The rules of the game do not only apply to the beauty of the moves but are also designed to allow the matador to get himself out of trouble. The very essence of bullfighting, the apex of the art, is the move "*al natural.*" But there are other more substantial moves, including those that the matador uses to get out of trouble.

A bullfighter punishing a wild bull from below performs in the ring on foot. A fired-up bullfighter lances the defeated head of the bull with masterly movements using the red cape. Some very exciting moves have been executed with very difficult bulls.

The matador dedicates the bull…

And if it is *pastueño*, at best he makes a display of prolonging the series of

moves by executing the *pase cambiado*, an extremely risky move: he incites the bull with the red cape gathered up in his left hand, the bull charges, and at the crucial moment he makes it alter its course by passing the cape to the other side and leaping away from the danger.

There are other ways of executing the *pase cambiado*, using the shoulder or inciting the bull with the right hand.

Estaturarios and the *ayudados* are other elegant ways of starting off a good series of moves with the red cape. And if in these moves the bull shows resilience, the bullfighter will immediately switch the red cape to his left hand.

The "*natural*" pass is the height of the art of bullfighting. These moves are executed with the left hand; the left hand is so important in bullfighting that seasoned aficionados called it "*la mano de los billetes*," ("the hand that grasps the bills").

It is an old saying that a great sequence of passes is worth the price of a country house. And indeed, after a great fight matadors who were previously little known or were past their peak, or who were not big names at all, would suddenly be showered with professional invitations.

Madrid used to be the most auspicious bullring in this respect. To be chaired into the ring in triumph through the *puerta grande*, known as the *puerta de Madrid*, on a single occasion was tantamount to a passport to glory.

The red cape in his left hand, the matador stands slightly at an angle to the bull, with the leg nearest to it set forward. Incited by the cape, the bull charges and as it lowers its head to butt it, the matador follows through by stepping forward on the other leg. This is exactly what happens with the *verónica* except that now the sword comes into play.

The *natural* pass at this stage of the fight must be succeeded by a second and then a third, three *naturals* being followed by one *de pecho*. The sequence is then repeated. A few times is sufficient. Three sets of *naturals* practically complete the phase.

A great phase can be performed with a very few passes if these are properly executed. A couple of dozen are enough. Neither the bull—which will be on the point of exhaustion—nor the crowd—on the edge of their seats—will respond to any more clever turns.

The most memorable series of passes that I can remember never went on for more than four minutes. Today's matadors make a feature of interminably long series of passes; even after a warning they will still continue. There is no question that these extenuated passes lead to victory, but this is more through quantity than quality. After ten minutes no bull will go on charging in response to moves executed thoroughly and in quick succession. If it does go on charging, this is because the passes are superficial and feeble, and perhaps do not run on continuously. They are thus considered to be of little worth.

The *natural* move will not exhaust the bull. Bullfighting with the cape has a wide repertoire. The cape may be held to the left; being a minor move this is the one most commonly used by today's bullfighters, and is very different from the rich sequence of passes devised by many masters in the long history of bullfighting.

The pass using both hands to hold the cape can be *por alto* (above) or *por bajo* (below). The pass *por bajo* is a recent development, known in the crowd as *dobladas* or *doblones* (doubles), emphasizing the bravery demanded by the move, since the bullfighter makes the bull lower its head and come round again. A very effective variation on this move when the bull is to be dominated is that known as *trinchera*, *trincherilla*, or *trincherazo*.

Whether using one or both hands, bullfighting requires skill. One hand is used in execution of the *natural*, the red cape held in the left hand, the sword in the right, and in the execution of the *derechazo*, when the red cape and the sword are held in the right hand. The right hand is also involved in the *trincherilla*, the *pase de pecho*, the *molinete*, the *afarolada*, and a whole range of daring moves, which include the *manoletina*, the *arrucina*, and many others.

Changes of hand mark shifts in the stages of a bullfight, and can be executed in front of the body, over the shoulder, or in almost any way.

The *pase de tirón* is used to close in on the bull and to give it space, if it shows signs of flagging. This pass is one that can be executed above, in front, over the shoulders, or at the side; passes of this type are named for their inventors.

Speaking of names, these can be misleading. For example, the *manoletina* was not invented by Manolete. The *pase de las flores*, invented by Victoriano de la Serna, an enormously charismatic bullfighter of the 1930s, was originally known as the *pase fallero* because he thought of performing it in a bullfight at the Fallas, the festival of San José in Valencia. It is in fact a version of the *manolete* and Ruano Llopis used it as a great crowd-puller, embellishing it with a garland of flowers. The move so impressed the crowd that it came to be known as the *pase de las flores* (pass of the flowers).

Moves with a repertoire attached are wonderful to see. Moves in which the bullfighter uses different tactics according to the condition of the bull or as inspiration takes him are the zenith of the art of bullfighting.

But moves are incomplete unless they culminate in a great sword thrust. Bulls were originally killed when they were received by the matador. When the *volapié* (running sword thrust) was invented, this way of dispatching the bull became so common that it was practically the only way for it to be done.

The bullfighter who, in my opinion, has best executed the *suerte de recibir*, the move in which the man stands still and receives the bull, is Rafael Ortega. The same goes for the *volapié*. Of all the post-Civil War matadors, Rafael Ortega has been the most skillful ever with the sword, having the ability to dispatch the bull with perfectly judged strength and great calmness. In one of the greatest bullfights that I have ever seen, back in the 1970s at the Feria de San Isidro, Rafael Ortega was the matador. Paradoxically, on that occasion he did not kill the bull as cleanly as usual, since it turned back on him after he had stabbed it; he was honored by receiving the two ears. That exciting bullfight, nothing short of an historic moment, caused a great commotion in the crowd. Some aficionados were practically in tears. This is the nobility of bullfighting.

Nevertheless, bullfighting also has its tragedies. A few minutes after the end of the fight, while the crowd were still in uproar, the bull fought by Curro Romero— a great friend of the master of San Fernando—was taken back to the corral alive. The insult turned into a story that never died down. The next day, every newspaper had the Curro story on the front page; reporters were given free rein to make a major splash with the affair, describing how Curro had been detained, what he said, and what the opinion of the authorities was.

Bullfighting, which evolved to dominate *Bos taurus primigenius*, who wandered freely in the leafy groves of the Iberian peninsula, has become a science known as tauromaquia. It has a stormy history formed of generosity and injustice, of bravery and failure, art and vulgarity, tragedy and glory. Bullfighters who have met their death on the horns of a bull, plus those who have had to retire after a goring, are numbered in their thousands. Those who took up the profession of bullfighter and had to give it up without achieving success are numbered in their tens of thousands. Those who have achieved moderate fame are numbered in the hundreds. Those who were the bullfighters of their day are numbered at hardly more than a dozen. And that is over a period of more than three hundred years.

Art and bravery, blood and sand—this is the most impressive spectacle in the entire world.

Lunwerg Editors would like to thank the following:

BULLRINGS
Albacete, Alicante, Aranjuez, Arganda del Rey, Benidorm, Bilbao,
Boadilla del Monte, Buitrago de Lozoya, Cáceres, Cercedilla, Chinchón,
Ciempozuelos, Colmenar de Oreja, Cuéllar, El Castañar de Béjar,
El Puerto de Santa María, Granada, Jerez de la Frontera,
La Glorieta de Salamanca, La Malagueta de Málaga,
Las Virtudes de Santa Cruz de Mudela, Murcia, Pamplona,
Plaza Monumental de Barcelona, Real Maestranza de Ronda,
Real Maestranza de Sevilla, Segovia, Sotillo de la Adrada,
Talavera de la Reina, Toledo, Valencia, Valladolid,
Vejer de la Frontera, and Zaragoza.

STOCKBREEDERS
Dolores Aguirre Ibarra, Ganadería de Concha y Sierra,
Ganadería de El Jaral de la Mira, Ganadería de La Laguna,
Ganadería de Torrestrella, Herederos de Gabriel Hernández Plá,
Herederos de Baltasar Ibán Valdés, Hijos de Celestino Cuadri,
Hijos de Eduardo Miura, Marqués de Albaserrada,
Victorino Martín Andrés, and Apolinar Soriano.

THE ESCUELA TAURINA DE MADRID
A Porfirio Enríquez, José Luis García-Palacios Álvarez,
José Carlos Valenciano and his wife, Víctor Puerto, Manuel Reyes,
the matadors, bullfighters, bullfighters' assistants, agents, managers,
and all those people who have made possible
the publication of this book.